International Marketing & Business English

Corey Allen Ross
Kap Soo Heo

International Marketing and Business English

도서출판 청람

Preface

Easy International Marketing and Business English is a textbook written for a classroom setting that encourages verbal interaction between students and the teacher. Many textbooks available have been written with the sole purpose of promoting an understanding of grammar with key vocabulary words while neglecting the importance of formal verbal communication. This book attempts to help teachers promote speaking within the classroom via pronunciation practice, spoken grammar drills, reading comprehension, verbal discussion of articles, and a variety of conversation topics. Many key words and issues throughout the book target the unique issues Koreans may struggle with when learning English or may be concerned with regarding marketing and business in the workplace, during travel, or simply in their own society.

The book is divided into 18 lessons that are further divided into two parts. Each lesson can be tailored for a class that lasts 2 to 3 hours, or each part can be taught in a class lasting 1 to 1.5 hours.

Students should be divided into pairs in order to help each other with the drills and conversations. The teacher should explain each section and allow time for the students to work through the various sections of the text using spoken English rather than writing answers down.

Proverbs and Idioms: (10 to 20 minutes per lesson) Each lesson presents a proverb and idiom for the students to learn. These should be introduced to the students and the usage of them explained. Teachers can expand on these by challenging students to use them in their conversation groups.

Pronunciation: (20 to 30 minutes per lesson) The teacher should go over the method to pronounce each sound presented in the lesson. This should then be followed by the teacher saying each word twice with students repeating each time. To break up the monotony, the teacher may stop on various words and ask the class to explain the meaning of the word in English, as many words are common or useful for retention. During the discussion time, the teacher can walk through the groups and check the pronunciation of the sound while the students are using them for drills or during conversation. This can help the students to perfect the sound during practical use rather than when specifically called upon.

Drills: (40 to 60 minutes per lesson) Grammar practice is offered using examples to show the format of the drill and a key that will cue the appropriate answer. Students can quiz each other and check each other, while the teacher checks each group to confirm students are answering appropriately. To check for understanding, the teacher can ask the students to close the book and then confirm understanding by calling out the key word or phrase for the students to answer together or individually. Various articles are also presented to help with reading comprehension of a variety of business and marketing topics. Teachers are encouraged to allow students to utilize their dictionaries to promote understanding.

Conversations: (50 to 70 minutes per lesson) Each lesson presents a business, marketing, and/or small talk related topic. There are twenty questions with sample answers to help students formulate their own answers. Students should be encouraged to substitute words and phrases to tailor the samples to their own unique circumstances. Conversation tests are offered in the appendix. These tests provide key word hints for the questions that can be used each class to help students practice question grammar recall and their answers. The final conversation topic in the book provides open ended discussion questions that may be used for a final term paper or a class presentation.

Contents

Lesson 03

Lesson 04

Lesson 05

Lesson 11

Lesson 12

Lesson 18

Appendix

Lesson 01

Pronunciation

Part I : /p/

Part II : /f/

Drills

Part I : Self Introduction

Substitution – "May I...", "Could I...", & "Can I..."

Part II : Substitution – "I like..."

Substitution – my major

Essay Example – self introduction

Conversations

Part I : Introduction

Part II : Extended Introduction

1

Part I

Today's Proverb

"When it rains, it pours."

Vocabulary Words

Trade, Distribution, Business Administration, Management

Pronunciation

/p/: People

Practice this sound several times in front of a mirror. Make sure that your lips start together when you make a /p/. Remember that the middle and the end /p/ are softer than the beginning /p/.

Beginning	Middle	End
people	complex	cap
product	opposite	trip
price	open	laptop
place	simple	group
passion	hopes	pop
promotion	hospital	jump

1. Most hospitals provide wireless Internet for patients with a laptop.
2. Poor people hope that they can take trips too.
3. Do you drink pop and eat pickles with your pizza?
4. Some stores promote ripe apples as their preferred product.
5. People are important parts of marketing strategy.
6. The salesperson placed a pen on my paper.

Drills

Drill #1: Introducing Yourself in English

[Formal Introduction] – (using Mr., Ms., Miss, and Mrs.)

A) Hello, Nice to meet you. My name is John Smith.

B) Hello, Mr. Smith. I'm Sun-Hee Choi.

A) It's a pleasure to meet you, Ms. Choi.

[Informal Introduction] – (to be on a first-name basis)

A) Hi, I'm George.

B) I'm Linda.

A) Nice to meet you, Linda.

B) Nice to meet you too, George.

*** Now introduce yourself to other students ***

Drill #2: Substitution Drill

(Using "May I...", "Could I...", or "Can I...")

NOTE: "Can I..." is more casual than the other two.

Key	Answer
Look at your paper.	*May I look at your paper?*
Read the dialogue.	*Could I read the dialogue?*
Ask me a question.	*Can I ask a question?*

1. Answer the question.	1. … answer the question.
2. Write the sentence.	2. … write the …
3. Listen carefully.	3. …
4. Repeat after me.	4. …
5. Don't use your dictionary.	5. …
6. Don't answer your cell phone.	6. …
7. Turn over your paper.	7. …
8. Raise your hand.	8. …
9. Do number six.	9. …
10. Stand up.	10. …
11. Turn in your test.	11. …
12. Work together.	12. …
13. Speak English.	13. …

*** Now review using 'please' in the sentence. (ex. Look at your paper, please.)***

Conversations

Conversation: Introduction

*** Answers a) and b) are examples. Please create your own answers. ***

1. Good afternoon. How are you today?
   a) I'm great.
   b) I'm a little tired.

2. What's your name?
   a) I'm ___________.
   b) My name is _____________.

3. What university do you attend?
   a) I attend the Catholic University of Pusan.
   b) I am attending this university, and I will graduate soon.

4. How many are there in your family?
   a) There are four in my family; my mother, my father, my older sister, and me.
   b) There are only two in my family. I live with my mother.

5. What are your hobbies?
   a) I really like baseball. It is my favorite hobby.
   b) I enjoy reading, singing, and watching movies with my friends.

6. Why did you take this class?
   a) I want to improve my English ability.
   b) I heard it was a good class.

7. Where do you live?
   a) I live in Busan with my family.
   b) I live alone in a studio apartment.

8. How old are you?
   a) I'm 21 years old.
   b) I don't want to tell you my age.

9. What's your favorite restaurant?
   a) My favorite restaurant is McDonald's. I love hamburgers.
   b) I really like KFC. They have great fried chicken.

10. What's your favorite kind of music?
    a) My favorite kind of music is rock and roll.
    b) I'm really into hip hop and dance music.

11. Where are you from?
    a) I'm from Korea.
    b) I'm from Busan, South Korea.

12. How did you come here today?
    a) I walked from my apartment. I will walk home too.
    b) I took the subway. It takes about 30 minutes for me to get here by subway.

13. What's your favorite kind of Korean food?
    a) I really love kimbop. I always eat it because it's cheap.
    b) I enjoy eating spicy food, so my favorite food is kimchi jigae.

14. Are you happy today?
    a) Yes, I am. I am very happy today.
    b) No, I'm very stressed. I just want to go home and rest.

15. Do you like to play sports?
    a) No, I just like watching them on TV.
    b) Sure, I always play soccer if I have a chance.

16. How many children do you want to have?
    a) I want to have 3 children.
    b) I don't want any children. I want to live alone.

17. What is your major?
    a) My major is business administration.
    b) I am majoring in accounting.

18. Tell me about your best friend.

19. Can you tell me how to get to the subway station from here?

20. What do you usually do on the weekends?

Part Ⅱ

Today's Idiom

"... (to be) no bed of roses."

(ex. "Studying English is no bed of roses.")

Pronunciation

/f/: Finance

One way to practice a good /f/ sound is to make sure your teeth are showing and to make a long and continuous /f/.

Beginning	Middle	End
finance	often	yourself
find	effort	staff
fight	affluent	laugh
forget	after	stuff
friend	offer	if
familiar	emphasize	brief

1. Fighting for your freedom is worth the effort.
2. Affluent friends can often forget to do their finances.
3. Laughing briefly can feel fantastic after a failure.
4. I often find myself eating fast before I go to school.
5. Fruit found in the office is offered to fantastic clients.
6. Students often forget that "elevator" is "lift" in British English.

Drills

Drill #1: Substitution Drill

(I like...)

Key	Answer
apples	*I like apples.*
strawberries	*I like strawberries.*
studying	*I like studying.*

1. reading	1. I … reading.
2. dancing	2. … like dancing.
3. watching TV	3. I like …
4. singing	4. …
5. sleeping	5. …
6. to read	6. …
7. to sing	7. …
8. to watch movies	8. …
9. to play sports	9. …
10. to go to school	10. …
11. to eat fast food	11. …
12. doing homework	12. …
13. speaking English	13. …
14. learning languages	14. …
15. drinking coffee	15. …

Drill #2: Substitution Drill

(my major)

Key	Answer
marketing	*I'm a marketing major.*
accounting	*I'm an accounting major.*
art	*I'm an art major.*

1. engineering	1. I'm an engineering …
2. law	2. I'm a … major.
3. management	3. I'm a …
4. English	4. … an …
5. business administration	5. …
6. biology	6. …
7. music	7. …
8. chemistry	8. …
9. nursing	9. …
10. geology	10. …
11. Japanese	11. …
12. public affairs	12. …
13. information technology	13. …
14. distribution management	14. …
15. radiology	15. …

Drill #3: Essay Example

(Self Introduction)

My name is Andrew. I am 23 years old. I am studying at the Catholic University of Pusan, and I am majoring in marketing. I live in Busan, South Korea with my family. There are four people in my family; my mother, father, older sister, and me. My older sister is married, but she has no children. She lives with her husband in Seoul. My mother and father are retired. I am planning to finish school and get a job working in the marketing department of a large company. These days, I spend my free time playing soccer with my friends and studying English. I am considering going abroad for one year to improve my English, but I'm not sure where I want to go yet.

Comprehension Questions:

1. What is his name?
2. How old is he?
3. What university does he attend, and what is his major?
4. Tell me about his family.

5. What are his plans after he finishes school?
6. What is he doing these days?
7. Where does he want to go to study English?

*** Extra Practice: Introduce yourself in a way similar to the essay. ***

Conversations

Conversation: Extended Introduction

1. Do you want to get a good score in this class?
   a) Yes, I do. I think I can get a good score in this class.
   b) Yeah, but I think it will be hard. I hope the teacher will help us.

2. What did you do yesterday afternoon?
   a) Nothing special. I just stayed at home and watched TV.
   b) I went to class, and I had to study for my next exam.

3. What are you going to do tomorrow morning?
   a) I'm going to get up early and eat breakfast.
   b) I plan to go to bed late, so I will sleep in tomorrow morning.

4. Do you have any friends in this class?
   a) Yes, I do. My friend is sitting over there.
   b) No, I don't. I want to meet some new friends in this class.

5. What do you do on the weekends?
   a) I usually spend my weekends at home studying.
   b) I like to go out to a karaoke box to sing with my friends.

6. Where did you eat lunch today?
   a) I ate kimchi and rice in the school cafeteria today.
   b) I didn't eat lunch today because I was too busy. I'll eat after class.

7. How do you study English?
   a) I study English by singing pop songs in English. I like American pop music.
   b) I really love C.S.I., and I watch it every day. Watching TV shows in English is helpful.

8. Where did you buy those shoes?
   a) I bought these shoes at Lotte Department Store. They were a good price.
   b) I ordered them from an online shopping mall.

9. Do you like to surf the Internet?
   a) Yes, I do. Surfing the Internet is my favorite hobby.
   b) Sometimes, I do. I only surf the Internet when I'm bored.

10. Do you like meeting new people?
    a) Yes, I do. I'm really outgoing.
    b) No, I don't. I'm too shy to meet new people.

11. Do you like going to the beach?
    a) Yes, I do. Haeundae Beach is the best in Korea.
    b) No, I don't. I really like going to the mountain instead.

12. What kinds of products do you like to buy?
    a) I like to buy makeup. I really like finding the perfect color for me.
    b) I like buying new clothes. I am interested in new styles and trends.

13. Where is your favorite Korean restaurant?
    a) My favorite Korean restaurant is near the subway station. It's called "Kimbop Chungook".
    b) My favorite restaurant is "Yoo Gah Nae". There is a good one near Pusan National University.

14. Who is your favorite actor/actress?
    a) My favorite actor is Johnny Depp. Have you seen "Pirates of the Caribbean"?
    b) Tae Hee Kim is my favorite actress. She was great in the drama "Iris".

15. What do you want to talk about in this class?

16. Who is your favorite professor?

17. Where do you usually study?

18. What is your favorite snack?

19. Tell me about your family.

20. What country would you like to travel to?

Extra Practice:

– Review the previous questions with your group, or ask new questions.

– Practice your self introduction.

Lesson 02

Pronunciation

Part Ⅰ : /p/ & /f/

Part Ⅱ : /b/

Drills

Part Ⅰ : Substitution – question, statement, negative, & affirmative

Substitution – pronouns + be

Part Ⅱ : Substitution – singular & plural nouns

Article – How to Perform a SWOT Analysis

Conversations

Part Ⅰ : General Questions

Part Ⅱ : Shopping

Part I

Today's Proverb

"A rolling stone gathers no moss."

Pronunciation

/p/ and /f/: Pair - Fair

A review of Lesson 1's pronunciation through minimal pairs.

Beginning	Middle	End
pair - fair	sipped - sift	tip - tiff
passion - fashion	ripped - rift	P.I.P. - P.I.F.F.*
pool - fool	raptor - rafter	lap - laugh
pun - fun	supper - suffer	goop - goof
peel - feel	upend - offend	cup - cuff
pill - fill	puppy - puffy	gulp - gulf

* P.I.F.F. has changed to B.I.F.F. (Busan International Film Festival)

1. I bought a pair of fantastic purple pants for my wife.
2. Many people come to see films at the Pusan International Film Festival.*
3. Peter fanned his friend while she sipped a cup of tea and laughed.
4. Five pieces of paper were ripped in half by the happy staff.
5. If you peel apples for friends, they will appreciate it.
6. Great effort provides you with a plan to avoid failure and suffering.

Drills

Drill #1: Substitution Drill

(question / statement / negative / affirmative)

Key	Answer
Is he a teacher?	*Is he a teacher?*
(statement)	*He is a teacher.*
(negative)	*He isn't (is not) a teacher.*
(affirmative)	*He is a teacher.*

1. (question)	Is he a teacher?
2. biologist	…
3. I	Am I a biologist?
4. you	Are…
5. flight attendant	…
6. (statement)	You are a flight attendant.
7. taxi driver	…
8. he	He is…
9. we	… taxi drivers.
10. I	… am a …
11. (negative)	I'm not a taxi driver.
12. professor	I'm not …
13. she	She's …
14. they	… not professors.
15. you	…
16. (affirmative)	You're a professor.
17. lawyer	…
18. I	…
19. she	…
20. we	…

Drill #2: Substitution Drill

(subject pronouns + be)

Key	Answer
She is tired.	*She is tired.*
(question)	*Is she tired?*
you	*Are you tired?*
(negative)	*Aren't you tired?*
(affirmative)	*Are you tired?*

1. sleepy	Are you sleepy?
2. (negative)	Aren't ...
3. he	...
4. (statement)	...
5. bored	He isn't bored.
6. (affirmative)	He's ...
7. they	...
8. I	...
9. happy	I am happy.
10. we	...
11. (question)	...
12. kind	...
13. (negative)	...
14. you	Aren't you kind?
15. (statement)	You aren't ...
16. she	...
17. angry	...
18. (affirmative)	She is angry.
19. I	...
20. they	...
21. (question)	Are they angry?
22. unkind	...
23. (negative)	...
24. he	...
25. (statement)	He isn't unkind.
26. she	...
27. (affirmative)	She is unkind.

28. I	…
29. we	…
30. you	You are unkind.

Conversations

Conversation: General Questions

1. Who is your favorite movie star?

   a) My favorite movie star is Brad Pitt.

   b) Julia Roberts is my favorite movie star.

2. Who is your best friend?

   a) My best friend is Ji-hyeon.

   b) Jin-soo is my best friend.

3. Who is the most famous soccer player in Korea?

   a) Ji-seong Park is the most famous soccer player in Korea.

   b) The most famous soccer player in Korea is Sung-yong Gi.

4. Where do you live?

   a) I live in Haeundae in Busan.

   b) I live near the Catholic University of Pusan.

5. Where is the library?

   a) It is next to the school cafeteria.

   b) It is in front of this building.

6. Where do you want to live in Korea?

   a) I want to live near this university.

   b) I want to live in Busan.

7. Where is a big department store in this city?
   a) There is a huge department store near the art museum.
   b) I know there is one large department store in Seomyun.

8. Where do you usually study?
   a) I usually study in my house. It's the most convenient.
   b) I usually go to the library to study because it's quiet.

9. Where did you go yesterday?
   a) I went to Seomyeon with my friends. We ate lunch together.
   b) I visited my grandmother in Ulsan.

10. What will you do tomorrow?
   a) I'll stay home all day long and study English.
   b) I will get together with my high school friends.

11. What is your favorite ice cream?
   a) My favorite ice cream is vanilla ice cream.
   b) I like cherry ice cream most.

12. What did you eat for lunch today?
   a) I ate a sandwich.
   b) I had lunch in the cafeteria. We ate rice and soup.

13. What will you eat for dinner tonight?
   a) I will eat some pizza with my family.
   b) I will have rice and fish with side dishes.

14. What time do you get up?
   a) I usually get up around 7:20 a.m.
   b) I get up at 7 o'clock on weekdays.

15. What time do you usually go to bed?

16. When will you go home today?

17. Where will you go after this class?

18. When will you see your best friend again?

19. When do you turn off your cell phone?

20. When do you want to travel?

Part II

Today's Idiom:

"...period."

(ex. "I'm not going to drink any soju tonight, period.")

Pronunciation

/b/: Basic

The /b/ sound is basically identical to /p/ but use your voice.

Beginning	Middle	End
basic	barbells	subscribe
brand	harbor	grab
book	labor	club
borrow	table	job
business	cabinet	dub
bored	distribute	Youtube

1. A basic understanding of brand image is important for business.
2. May I borrow your book because I'm bored.
3. You can buy soap bars and bubble bath soap in "Bath and Beauty".
4. Subscribe to Youtube channels to learn about hobbies.
5. I'd better go to the bookstore to apply for a job.
6. Billy went abroad before he met his bride.

Drills

Drill #1: Substitution Drill

(singular/plural nouns)

Key	Answer
The apple is red.	*The apple is red.*
apples	*The apples are red.*
delicious	*The apples are delicious.*

Key	Answer
1. is	The apple is delicious.
2. sweet	The apple is …
3. (question)	… apple sweet?
4. it	Is ...
5. the oranges	Are …
6. sour	… sour?
7. (statement)	The oranges are sour.
8. they	… sour.
9. it	…
10. fresh	It's …
11. the vegetables	… fresh.
12. (negative)	… aren't …
13. they	…
14. (affirmative)	…
15. salty	…
16. it	…
17. (question)	… salty?
18. the fish	Is the fish…?
19. (negative)	Isn't …
20. (statement)	… isn't salty.
21. the French fries	…
22. (affirmative)	… are …
23. they	…
24. burned	They are …
25. the steak	…
26. (negative)	…
27. the steaks	… burned.

28. it	… isn't…
29. they	They … burned.
30. (affirmative)	…. are …

Drill #2: Article

How to Perform a SWOT Analysis

A SWOT analysis is one way for an organization to understand where it stands in an existing market. By analyzing a firm's current strong points, weak points, opportunities for improvement, and threats, managers can gain a better understanding of how to develop strategy for continued or future success for the firm.

SWOT stands for strengths, weaknesses, opportunities, and threats. Strengths and weaknesses of an organization are the internal factors that can be controlled through various management strategies, such as the 4P's. (Lesson 6 will provide a more in-depth look at the 4P's.) Opportunities and threats are external factors that influence a company due to the environment it is operating in, such as the competition, current trends, and economic conditions of consumers. When first preparing a SWOT analysis, it may be useful to make a table or a simple list rather than focusing in detail on each individual point carefully.

For instance, when considering a major corporation, such as Samsung, we could make the following SWOT: The strengths would include innovation, design, marketing, brand image, smartphone sales, etc. The weaknesses would be low profit margin, lack of its own smartphone operating system, too many product versions, etc. The opportunities might consist of better expansion into the tablet market, bringing more devices to India and China, development of its own operating system, etc. And, Samsung's threats include Apple, LG, a technology market that is constantly changing and upgrading, too many smartphones companies and versions, competitive pricing, and patent issues.

Strengths

Strengths are factors that you can control within your company. They are beneficial to your company and can be both tangible and intangible. Some questions you might ask to determine your strengths are "What are the competitive advantages that my company has compared to other companies?", "What are we very effective at?", and "What are some of the main reasons our customers like us?".

Strengths can be many things, such as marketing strategies, financial power of the company, the excellence of the sales force, and more. You will need to decide what attributes in your company are your strong points and what will give you a competitive advantage over your rivals.

Weaknesses

Weaknesses are factors that are within your business. They are often able to be controlled by effective management. They can be any factor that limits your company's ability to achieve or maintain a competitive edge and are something that should be considered for improvement.

Weaknesses can be anything from lack of knowledge, inferior technology or technological skills, a bad location, mismanagement, or a poor brand image. While these various factors might be controllable, it may be difficult to implement changes that can reduce these weaknesses. Weaknesses can ultimately damage the value of your product or service and can allow for competition to enter the market or even put you out of business.

Opportunities

Opportunities are factors that exist outside of your company that could be a good way for your company to grow and succeed. These factors are chances for your company that you are currently not taking advantage of. Opportunities for your company can come about from new trends in the market, changes in brand image, the loss of a big competitor, or consumer lifestyle changes.

In order to succeed in the dog eat dog world of business, your company will need to constantly analyze new opportunities and determine if your company can capitalize on their existence. While opportunities will almost always exist, it may not always be feasible to try to pursue them. Effective managers will need to be critical of which opportunities present the best possible chances of success for a new project or business venture.

Threats

Threats are factors that are present in the environment in which your company operates in but can also be from within the company itself. This means that threats can be nearly anything that could cause damage to your company's well-being. For instance, a threat can be an unfavorable trend in the market or a new law passed by the government restricting your company's former freedoms. Competition, whether an existing rival or just a chance for a new business to enter the market, is always a threat that must be analyzed carefully. While some threats are not controllable, it may be useful to have a strategic plan to deal with threats to the best of your company's ability. These backup plans could save your company from failure if the worst case scenario were to happen.

In today's modern market, technology is advancing at a very fast pace. Many companies are often at risk of falling behind and becoming obsolete or forgotten. Other times, companies can find themselves in a "leap frog" race for who has the most advanced tech gadget on the market, such as the smartphone wars between Apple and Samsung. Even industries that were once safe from technological advances, such as bookstores and music stores, have been increasingly threatened by digital versions of their products.

Conversations

Conversation: Shopping

1. Do you like to go shopping?
   a) Yes, I do. I love to go shopping.
   b) No, I don't. Shopping is boring.

2. Where do you usually go to buy your clothes?
   a) I usually go to Nampo–dong to buy my clothes.
   b) I order my clothes on the Internet.

3. Do you like online shopping?
   a) Yes, I do. I usually buy clothes from online shopping malls.
   b) No, I don't. I can't see the products, so I don't want to buy them.

4. Which site do you usually use for online shopping?
   a) I usually shop at www.gmarket.co.kr.
   b) I like www.interpark.co.kr for books.

5. What is your favorite clothing brand?
   a) My favorite brand is Nike. I like sportswear.
   b) I don't care about the brand name. I just buy whatever looks nice.

6. Who do you usually go shopping with?
   a) I go shopping with my friends.
   b) I like to go shopping alone.

7. How often do you go shopping?
   a) I shop every week.
   b) I go shopping once a month.

8. Where is a good place to shop in this city?
   a) Lotte Department store is great for shopping.
   b) There are many kinds of stores in Nampo–dong.

9. Are you good at getting a deal?
   a) Yes, I am. I always bargain well.
   b) No, I am not. I don't have enough patience to argue about the price.

10. Where do you buy your groceries?
    a) I usually buy them at E–mart.
    b) I buy food at a corner store on the way home from school.

11. Do you ever buy products in the subway?
    a) Yes, I do. I usually buy umbrellas when it's raining.
    b) No, I don't. I try to ignore the people selling something on the subway.

12. Which is better, a big supermarket or an outdoor, traditional market?
    a) I think traditional markets are better. They are cheaper.
    b) Big supermarkets are more efficient to shop in.

13. Do you sometimes buy junk food, like snacks or pop?
    a) Yes, I do. I always eat snacks and drink soda when I have a chance.
    b) No, I don't. I think junk food is bad for my health, so I try to avoid it.

14. What do you do before going shopping?
    a) I write down a shopping list.
    b) I search for the price on Internet.

15. Where is a good place to buy women's clothes?

16. Where is a good place to buy cheap shoes?

17. Where can I buy computer parts?

18. Where can I go shopping with a foreign friend?

19. Tell me about a gift you bought for your friend. Did your friend like it?

20. What foreign brand do you like to buy? Where do you buy it?

Extra Practice:

- Review the previous questions with your group, or ask new questions.
- Talk about some problems you've had while shopping.
- Have you ever had a bad experience with an online shopping mall?
- How can we make shopping more convenient?

Lesson 03

Pronunciation

Part I : /v/

Part II : /b/ & /v/

Drills

Part I : Q&A – condition and opinion + Questions
Substitution – personal qualities
Article – Pyramid of Learning

Part II : Q&A – to like & to be like
Article – Understanding the Needs of Consumers

Conversations

Part I : General Questions – How

Part II : Brand Awareness Questions

Part I

Today's Proverb

"All good things come to he who waits."

Pronunciation

/v/: Violin

It is important that you remember /v/ is the same as /f/ but with your voice. /v/ is a continuous sound, and your teeth should be visible during the sound.

Beginning	Middle	End
violin	advance	grave
victory	savor	believe
vie	movie	save
veil	television	conceive
value	convenience	live
vicarious	evasion	prove

1. Various families visit graves on Chuseok.
2. The five rivals invested their money in the movie industry.
3. I have a DVD player, a big TV, and a valuable vase.
4. The convenience store is not a place to find savings.
5. Everyone believes love can save our violent world.
6. The value of goods varies among individuals.

Drills

Drill #1: Q&A – Condition/Opinion Questions

(pronoun answers)

Key	Answer
How is your mother?	*She is fine.*
How is the dinner?	*It is delicious.*
1. How is your father?	He is …
2. How is your friend?	She is…
3. How are the apples?	They are…
4. How is the weather?	It is…
5. How is this class?	It is …
6. How is your computer?	…
7. How are your parents?	…
8. How is the music?	…
9. How are your friends?	…
10. How are the pies?	…
11. How is McDonald's?	…
12. How are you all?	…
13. How is your professor?	…
14. How is your sister?	…
15. How is your brother?	…
16. How is that restaurant?	…
17. How is the coffee?	…
18. How are you?	…
19. How is my look?	…
20. How is your apartment?	…
21. How are foreigners in Korea?	…
22. How is your cold?	…
23. How is your English?	…
24. How are the students?	…
25. How is your friend's family?	…
26. How are they?	…
27. How is the bathroom?	…
28. How is the weather in winter?	…

29. How are the flowers in spring?	...
30. How are you and your family?	...

Drill #2: Substitution Drill

(personal qualities)

Key	Answer
kind woman	*She is a kind woman.*
warm	*She is a warm woman.*
he	*He is a warm man.*

1. generous	He is a ... man.
2. optimistic	He is ... man.
3. cheerful	He ...
4. easy-going	...
5. unkind lady	... an unkind lady.
6. cold	... cold lady.
7. mean	... lady.
8. pessimistic	...
9. miserable	...
10. man	He ...
11. weak	...
12. honest	He is ... honest man.
13. clever	...
14. shy	...
15. good-looking	He is a good-looking ...
16. gentle	...
17. cute	...
18. woman	...
19. beautiful	She ...
20. lovely	...
21. sensitive	...
22. extroverted	... an extroverted woman.
23. lazy	...
24. introverted	...
25. hard-working	...

26. man	...
27. reliable	...
28. flexible	...
29. good	...
30. dishonest	...

Drill #3: Article

Pyramid of Learning

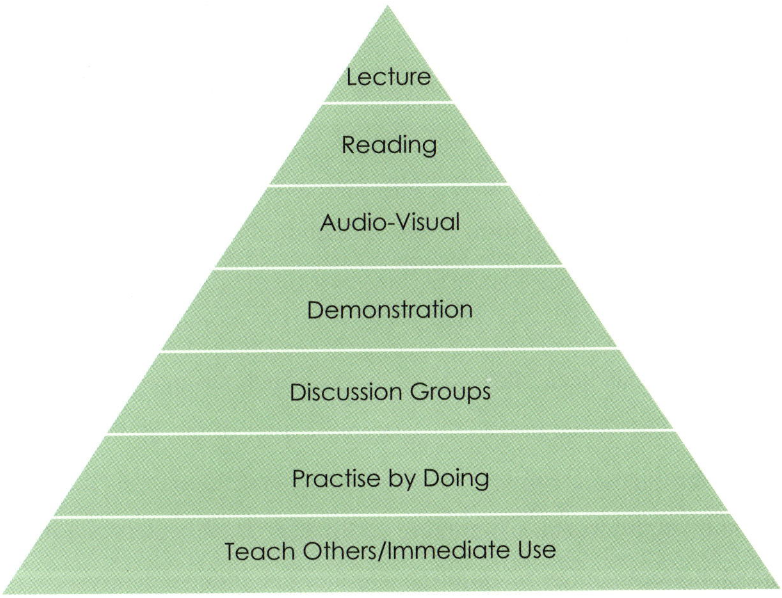

"What we have to learn to do, we learn by doing." – Aristotle

The Learning Pyramid is often used by teachers to help their students understand better ways to recall important information. While it may not be true in every scenario or for every individual, it is generally thought to be a useful model for learning. The higher portions of the triangle are passive learning methods with the learner only acquiring information from inputs but not interacting much. The lower portions of the triangle, which are the best for memory recall and retention, are active learning methods that require the learner to not only receive information but to generate information output in an effective manner.

Lecture

Listening to another person speak uses the smallest of the memory centers in the brain. When another is speaking, it is easy to be distracted or miss critical points.

Reading

Reading is the next step up from listening but suffers from the same problems as lectures. It is easy to become distracted or misunderstand the importance of various key points. Reading may help, but boredom and distraction often increase with the second and third times of reading the same thing.

Audio –Visual

Visual memory has been shown to give us a much stronger impression than audio memory. The visual part of the memory center of the brain is much larger. Humans are visual creatures and heavily depend upon sight for acquiring information from the world. Combining audio and visual centers is going to result in much better memory retention than either one independently.

Demonstration

Demonstrations include experiments, acting out scripts, or seeing something in action. In this stage, we can remember more information because our brain is not only acquiring information to remember but also attempting to process and interpret what we are seeing or experiencing.

Discussion Groups

Acting in a discussion group helps us to overcome misunderstanding through more active learning. Where the previous techniques were mainly passive learning methods, actively discussing things you should remember is a more hands–on approach to learning. When we are interacting, our brain begins engaging other portions beyond simple memory centers, which can ultimately help us with information retention and recall.

Practice by Doing

When we do something in order to remember it, our memory connects the information with the physical world. This gives us two ways to recall information since the information is married to an actual event. The old adage "practice makes perfect" is an important one to remember. Actively doing something can help to maintain an interest and engagement in the learning process. For instance, actually driving a car as a student driver improves our driving skill and understanding of laws much better than trying to memorize them from a book because we are experiencing them in a realistic setting, and it is somewhat exciting and a bit scary. This excitement gives us more motivation to learn and become better at what we are doing. Very few people like to be seen as a rookie forever.

Teach Others/Immediate Use

Teaching others requires us to have knowledge above those we are teaching. It requires us to be able to explain the information in several ways to others in order to help them understand the concept. Before we can ever explain something, we must fully understand it ourselves. The simple act of teaching can give us the motivation and pride for a standard of excellence that we would not normally try to reach. Also, immediately using acquired information in an actual setting can help to cement the information into our long term memory. When we do something, such as driving, immediately after studying it, we are putting our knowledge into practice and showing our brain that this knowledge is not something to be taken lightly, and instead, it should be saved in our long term memory.

Conversations

Conversation: General Questions – How

1. How do you study English?
   - a) I study TOEIC words every day.
   - b) I take an English class on Monday in my university.

2. How do you come to the university?
   - a) I take the subway and transfer to the shuttle bus.
   - b) I come here on foot. It is very close to my house.

3. How do you usually make new friends?
   - a) I usually talk to new people first.
   - b) I try to remember people's names.

4. How do you clean your room?
   - a) I use a vacuum cleaner. It is quite easy.
   - b) I sweep my room with a broom and wipe the floor with a wet cloth.

5. How do you usually spend your vacation?
   - a) I usually study English during my vacation.
   - b) I usually work during my vacation. I want to have some experience for my future job.

6. How are you?
   - a) I'm good. Thanks.
   - b) Just fine. Thanks for asking.

7. How do you feel today?
   a) I feel better than yesterday. I slept well last night.
   b) I don't feel good. I have a stomachache.

8. How are your parents?
   a) They are doing well.
   b) My mother had a small car accident recently, but she is ok now.

9. How will the weather be this evening?
   a) It will be cloudy.
   b) I heard it'll rain a little bit in the evening.

10. How are your classes this semester?
    a) They are a little difficult, but they are fun.
    b) They are easier than I thought.

11. How difficult are your classes?
    a) They're not difficult at all. I think I will do well this semester.
    b) They're pretty difficult, but I can get good scores if I preview the lessons every week.

12. How hard do you usually study?
    a) I go to the library every day to study.
    b) I don't study hard. I only study for tests.

13. How much do you like your name?
    a) I don't like my name. I think it is too plain.
    b) I really love my name. It is easy to remember.

14. How clean is city tap water?
    a) I'm not sure, so I have a water filter in my apartment.
    b) I think it is not clean to drink. I boil the tap water before drinking it.

15. How much do you miss your high school days?
    a) I don't miss my high school days. I only studied and didn't have much fun.
    b) I really miss my high school days. I had many good friends.

16. How do you find information for your studies?

17. How do you feel about the Korean president?

18. How do you hear about world news?

19. How do you usually contact your friends?

20. How do you hear about your old friends?

Part Ⅱ

Today's Idiom

"... a man of his word..."

(ex. "Jason is a man of his word.")

Pronunciation

/b/&/v/: (Boat – Vote)

A review of the /b/ and /v/ pronunciations through minimal pairing.

Beginning	Middle	End
boat - vote	hobble - hovel	curb - curve
bee - V	Serbs - serves	dub - dove
beer - veer	"lubber" - lover	robe - rove
ban - van	saber - saver	verb - verve
bowel - vowel	dribble - drivel	lib - live
berry - very	rabble - ravel	Deb - dev

1. Everyone bought valuable vases for Brenda's birthday.
2. You can leave the blue vest for my best man.
3. I served several bats some berries and bugs.
4. The various vans were blue, violet, and black.
5. Bob saved me from drowning in the big river.
6. Bath robes aren't as trendy as before.

Drills

Drill #1: Q&A – Two Uses of "Like"

(to like / to be like)

Key	Answer
What do you like?	*I like kimchi.*
What are you like?	*I am kind.*

1. What is your mother like?	...
2. What does your mother like?	...
3. What is Seoul like?	...
4. What do Seoulites like?	...
5. What are Seoulites like?	...
6. What do your parents like?	...
7. What are your parents like?	...
8. What is your phone like?	...
9. What is your best friend like?	...
10. What does your best friend like?	...

Drill #2: Article

Understanding the Needs of Consumers

It is important for marketers to comprehend the needs of consumers. This is not so easy, unfortunately, since consumers are often unable to articulate their specific needs and wants, and the consumers are sometimes unaware of what those needs and wants even are. For instance, before the advent of modern technological communication devices and methods, such as smartphones, the information superhighway (i.e. the Internet), social networking sites, email, etc., many individuals felt that they had no need for them and were slow to accept these things into their lives. When the computer was first sold to the public, people did not know how it could benefit their lives. So, the first personal computer companies, such as Apple, had to teach consumers how computers could benefit them. Commercials are one method used by companies to show potential consumers how to use new devices and how the use of the devices can improve day–to–day living. Today, society can hardly imagine what the world was like before the digital era.

In order for marketers to understand the minds of consumers, they must ask the right questions to learn about the consumers' needs and wants. This is no easy task, but effective marketing research can help marketers gather useful information. This information can then be used to formulate marketing strategies that will help a business to succeed with their product lines.

Comprehension Questions:

1. What is important for marketers to do?
2. Is understanding consumer needs easy? Why or why not?
3. Why were people slow to accept new technologies, such as the smartphone?
4. What was the problem when computers were first introduced to the public?
5. How did the first personal computer companies solve the problem?
6. What is "the digital era"?
7. How can effective marketing research help marketers?

Discussion Questions:

1. Which do you prefer, an Apple Computer or a PC?
2. What did you mainly use your first computer for?
3. How can we do marketing research?
4. Where can we learn about new tech devices?

Conversations

Conversation: Brand Awareness Questions

*** Ask your partner 1-5, 6-10, 11-15. (change the underlined words) ***

1. What is your favorite brand of clothing?
   a) My favorite clothing brand is Nike.
   b) I don't really have a favorite clothing brand, but I think Nike is a good brand.

2. Why do you like Nike clothes?
   a) They are very popular. Many famous people wear Nike clothes.
   b) I think Nike is higher quality than other brands.

3. Are you wearing any Nike clothes right now?
   a) Yes, my jacket is made by Nike.
   b) I am wearing Nike shoes right now. Look!

4. Is Nike expensive?
   a) Actually, Nike is quite expensive.
   b) I don't think Nike is very expensive. The price is reasonable because it's such a great quality product.

5. Where do you usually buy Nike clothes?
   a) I usually buy Nike clothes in Nampodong. There is a Nike store there.
   b) When I buy Nike clothes, I often shop online. I think online stores have the most variety.

6. What is your favorite fast food chain?
   a) I really love McDonald's. It's cheap, but very delicious.
   b) My favorite fast food chain is "Yoo–gah–nae" I love spicy chicken.

7. Where is one that is nearby?
   a) There is one located in Seomyun.
   b) I think there are several over by Pusan National University.

8. Tell me about the food there.
   a) They serve hamburgers, French fries, and ice cream. I really like their Big Macs.
   b) Their spicy dahk–galbi is the best. I always order that when I go there.

9. Do they have any special events or discounts?
   a) Yes, they do. You can use your "Ok Cashback Card" there.
   b) Sometimes, they do. Some of the restaurants will give you a mileage card.

10. When was the last time you went there?
    a) I went there last week with my friend. We bought hamburgers and fries.
    b) My family took me there yesterday. It was very crowded, so the service was too slow.

11. How often do you watch TV?
    a) I watch TV for one hour every day.
    b) I almost never watch TV because I have to study every night.

12. Who is your favorite TV personality?
    a) I really like Kang, Ho–dong. He's really funny.
    b) I don't have a favorite TV personality. But, I think Park, Myung–soo is pretty good.

13. Has your favorite TV personality been in any commercials?
   a) Yes, I think I saw him in a "Chon-dahk" commercial.
   b) I don't think I've seen him in any commercials.

14. Have you ever purchased a product because a TV star or singer was in the commercial?
   a) After I saw Psy in a ramyeon commercial, I bought it.
   b) I don't really buy something just because a TV star likes it.

15. Have you ever met a famous person and talked to him/her?
   a) No I haven't, I've never had a chance to meet a famous person.
   b) Yes, I have. I talked to Big Bang after a concert.

16. What is your favorite cell phone brand? Why?

17. Where can you buy cheap products?

18. Tell me about your favorite TV commercial.

19. Do you know any brand songs?

20. What is your favorite brand? Why do you like it so much?

Extra Practice:

- Review the previous questions with your group, or ask new questions.
- Discuss two different brands, like Coke and Pepsi. Why are they different? Which one do you prefer?
- Talk about some of the features on your cell phone.
- Have you ever bought a knock-off, such as an imitation Nike shirt?
- What is your favorite style of commercials: funny commercials, celebrity commercials, informative commercials, or stylish and fun commercials?

Lesson 04

Pronunciation

Part I : /l/

Part II : /r/

Drills

Part I : Substitution – jobs

Substitution – adjectives

Part II : Q&A – yes & no

Q&A – contrary adjectives

Article – The Service Recovery Paradox

Conversations

Part I : General Questions

Part II : Jobs

4

Part I

Today's Proverb

"Necessity is the mother of invention."

Vocabulary Words

employer, employee, boss/manager, supervisor

Pronunciation

/l/: Like

To make the /l/ sound, you have to put your tongue behind your teeth and not move your lips.

Beginning	Middle	End
like	lily	will
lips	silly	sell
laugh	belly	hassle
look	lollipop	call
listen	deli	nail
love	alone	role

1. I almost never listen to long love songs.
2. Exercise can help to reduce the size of a large belly.
3. He seldom laughs at life's difficulties.
4. Lily called about selling her leather jacket.
5. The employer usually likes to let people leave early.
6. I usually look at myself in the mirror when I'm lonely.

Drills

Drill #1: Substitution Drill

(jobs)

Key	Answer
Emma, accountant	*Emma is an accountant.*
(question)	*Is Emma an accountant?*
1. Madison, acrobat	... an acrobat?
2. Aaron, actor	... actor?
3. Emily, anchor woman	... an anchor woman?
4. Ethan, manager	Is Ethan a ...
5. (statement)	Ethan is a ...
6. Ryan, announcer	... is an announcer.
7. Isabella, editor	Isabella ...
8. Jack, bus driver	...
9. Joshua, movie director	...
10. Chloe, consultant	...
11. Logan, designer	...
12. (question)	... designer?
13. McKenna, counselor	Is ... ?
14. Kylie, chef	...
15. Benjamin, clerk	...
16. Elijah, cashier	...
17. (statement)	Elijah is ...
18. Ian, bartender	...
19. Daniel, athlete	Daniel is an ...
20. Colin, astronaut	...

Drill #2: Substitution Drill

(adjectives)

Key	Answer
nice boy	*He is a nice boy.*
You	*You are a nice boy.*
(question)	*Are you a nice boy?*
1. selfish	Are you ...
2. she	Is she ...
3. they	Are they ...
4. foolish	...
5. reckless	...
6. (statement)	They ...
7. Jenna	...
8. he	He is...
9. smart	...
10. thoughtless	...
11. (negative)	He isn't ... boy.
12. you	... aren't ..
13. good	...
14. (affirmative)	...
15. careful	You are a ...
16. they	... boys
17. (question)	... boys?
18. dangerous	Are they ... boys?
19. he	...
20. we	...

Conversations

Conversation: General Questions

1. Do you have a boyfriend/girlfriend?
   a) Yes, I do. We have been dating for two weeks.
   b) No, I don't. I am single.

2. Do you have any pets?
   a) Yes, I do. I have a dog. He's so cute.
   b) No, I don't. I have an allergy to pet fur.

3. What do you have in your bag?
   a) I have a cell phone and some books.
   b) I have a scarf and some lip gloss.

4. What kind of music MP3s do you have at home?
   a) I have some Korean rock music MP3s at home.
   b) I have classic music MP3s and Korean traditional music MP3s at home.

5. What do you usually do on the subway?
   a) I usually listen to music on the subway.
   b) I usually sleep or read a book on the subway.

6. Do you cook often?
   a) Yes, I do. I like to cook for my friends.
   b) No, I don't. I usually like to eat out.

7. Did you have any classes yesterday?
   a) Yes, I did. I had a math class yesterday.
   b) No, I didn't. I didn't have any classes yesterday.

8. Did you see a movie last weekend?

   a) Yes, I did. I saw "Avengers 2".

   b) No, I didn't. I had to visit my grandmother.

9. Do you ever dance in front of people?

   a) Yes, I do. I like to dance with my friends.

   b) No, I don't. I am not a good dancer.

10. Will you go shopping this weekend?

   a) Yes, I will. I really like to shop.

   b) No, I won't. I have to study this weekend.

11. How often do you go to a movie theater?

   a) I go to a movie theater once a month with my friend.

   b) I go to a movie theater almost every weekend to see action movies.

12. How often do you buy clothes?

   a) I buy clothes every month. I love shopping.

   b) I buy new clothes every season because I like trendy clothes.

13. How often do you play sports?
    a) I play soccer once a week at school.
    b) I almost never play sports.

14. How often do you go out to eat?
    a) I eat out almost every day with my family.
    b) I go out to eat once a week alone.

15. How many times do you send text messages every day?
    a) I send more than 10 text messages every day.
    b) I send 2 or 3 text messages every day.

16. How many countries have you visited?

17. How much time do you spend studying?

18. How much time do you spend exercising?

19. How many brothers and sisters do you have?

20. How many times do you take public transportation every day?

Part II

Today's Idiom

"... to drop the ball."

(ex. "Amy really dropped the ball on this one.")

Pronunciation

/r/: Radio

When you make the /r/ sound, you must not touch the top of your mouth with the tip of your tongue. Your tongue will make a spoon shape and the sound comes from deep in your mouth. /r/ makes two different sounds. 1) When /r/ is in the initial part of the syllable, your lips must move. 2) When /r/ is at the end of a syllable, it will make a continuous /–er/ sound and your tongue and lips will not move. /–er/ is very similar to the /eh/ sound, only slightly deeper in your mouth. NOTE: (re– / ear)

Beginning	Middle	End
radio	drama	bar
race	crayon	solar
rice	treasure	dollar
roller	correct	ear
rose	barrel	layer
read	ferret	air

1. Everyone was ready to roll the red barrels.
2. Bryan read the real story from the reporter's article.
3. The reckless girl was mean but pretty.
4. Roxanne still remembers her red dress.
5. The rabbits are eating carrots at Rebecca's farm.
6. I have never broken my ribs.

Drills

Drill #1: Q&A Drill

('yes' and 'no' answers)

Key	Answer
Tom, hardworking actor	*Is Tom a hardworking actor?*
Yes	*Yes, he's a very hardworking actor.*
No	*No, he's not a very hardworking actor.*
1. Sam, kind announcer	Is Sam a kind announcer?
2. Yes	Yes, he's a very ...
3. No	No, he's not a very ...
4. Isabella, skillful editor	... a skillful editor?
5. Yes	Yes, she's ... editor.
6. No	No, she's not ... editor.
7. Jack, lazy bus driver	Is ... driver?
8. Yes	Yes, he's ... driver.
9. No	No, he's not ... driver.
10. Chloe, successful consultant	Is Chloe ... ?
11. Yes	Yes, she's a ...
12. No	No, she's not a ...
13. Jenny, funny counselor	...
14. Yes	...
15. No	...
16. Benjamin, quiet clerk	...
17. Yes	...
18. No	...
19. Ethan, patient manager	...
20. Yes	...
21. No	...

Drill #2: Q&A Drill

(contrary adjectives)

Key	Answer
The cat - fat ***No - thin***	*Is the cat fat?* *No, it isn't a fat cat. It's a thin cat.*
Kang, Ho-dong - well-known comedian ***No - unknown***	*Is Kang, Ho-dong a well-known comedian?* *No, he isn't a well-known comedian. He is an unknown comedian*

1. this supermarket - cheap **2. No - expensive**	Is this ... cheap? No, it isn't a ... supermarket. It's an ... supermarket.
3. this car - dangerous **4. No - safe**	Is this ...? No, it ... car. It's a ...
5. the girl - tall **6. No - short**	Is ... ? No, she ... She's a ... girl.
7. this bag - heavy **8. No - light**	... No, ... It's a light bag.
9. these - strong windows **10. No - weak**	... ...
11. the teacher - strict **12. No - lenient**	... ...
13. the kids - good **14. No - bad**	... ...
15. he - mean clerk **16. No - nice**	... ...
17. the water - hot **18. No - cold**	... ...
19. it - dirty room **20. No - clean**	... ...

Drill #3: Article

The Service Recovery Paradox

The service recovery paradox occurs when customers become more loyal after a failure of a product or service. The reason for this occurrence is that excellent service recovery through proper handling of the failure situation ultimately results in the customer being more satisfied than if the failure had never happened in the first place. This means that an unsatisfied customers can be transformed into very loyal customers through effective service recovery.

So, since it seems that service failures with effective service recovery can improve a customer's loyalty, does that mean that a company should force a service failure just so that it can increase customer loyalty? This is why there is a paradox. As we know, having a reputation for failure is rarely good for a company's image. Service failure should never be a goal for any company. However, when a failure does happen, it presents an opportunity for increased customer satisfaction if handled correctly. It's important for companies to do their best to always provide top quality service as well as to help their customers with effective service recovery techniques when a failure does occur.

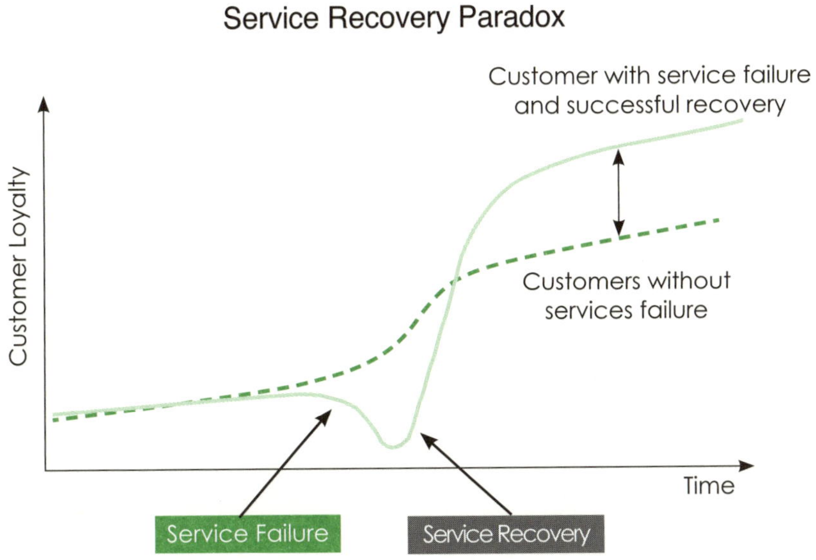

Discussion Questions:

1. Why is service recovery important?
2. Why are customers more loyal after a service failure and recovery?
3. Have you ever had a bad customer experience? How did the company solve your problem?
4. How do you feel when you experience a service failure?
5. How do you feel when you experience a service recovery?
6. What company in Korea has the best customer service?

Conversations

Conversation: Jobs

1. Have you ever had a job?
   a) Yes, I have. I worked in a factory during summer vacation.
   b) No, I haven't. I'd like to have a part time job soon.

2. How much is the minimum wage in Korea?
   a) It is 4,860 won per hour. I think it is small.
   b) I don't know. I think it is under 5,000 won per hour.

3. What part time job is the most popular for college students?
   a) I think working for a convenience store is the most popular.
   b) Working in a restaurant is the most popular because it is easy to find that kind of job.

4. Are you interested in doing an internship?
   a) Yes, I am. I will apply for an internship at Samsung.
   b) No, I'm not. I want to get a real job.

5. Which company do you want to work for?
   a) I'd like to work for LG.
   b) I want to work for a university.

6. What do you do to get a job?
   a) I study English to get good score on the TOEIC.
   b) I try to have part time jobs to improve my work experience.

7. What qualities do you want to have for your future jobs?
   a) I want to have good computer skills.
   b) I want to study foreign languages for my future jobs.

8. Do you think being a trader is a good job?
   a) Yes, I do. It is a stable job.
   b) No, I don't. It is a boring job and too hard to get.

9. What kind of job do you want to have?
   a) I want to work in a distribution center. I have good organizational skills.
   b) I want to start my own business. I'd like to open a restaurant.

10. What are your strong points?
   a) I am hardworking and kind.
   b) I learn faster than other people and make friends easily.

11. Do you want to work for a foreign company?
   a) Yes, I do. Foreign companies pay more than Korean ones.
   b) I don't care. I just want to have a good salary.

12. Do you want to work abroad?
   a) Yes, I do. I'd like to work in the U.S. to experience a new culture.
   b) No, I don't. I want to work in Korea to be near my family and friends.

13. Do you want to go to graduate school?
   a) Yes, I do. I need to study more for my future.
   b) No, I don't. I want to work as soon as I finish school.

14. What is the most important thing to consider when you choose a job?
    a) The salary is the most important thing to consider because we need money to live.
    b) The work schedule is the most important thing for me because I don't like stress.

15. Do you like to work in an office all the time?
    a) Yes, I do. I like to work in an office because I like computers.
    b) No, I don't. I sometimes want to work outside because I love nature.

[Role Play] Job Interview Questions:

(Please, pretend you are an interviewee. Choose a job you are applying for. For example: Public Official, University Lecturer, Salesman, etc.)

16. Please, introduce yourself.

17. Why are you applying for this job?

18. What do you consider most when you apply for a job?

19. What skills do you have for this job?

20. Tell me about your work experience.

Extra Practice:

- Review the previous questions with your group, or ask new questions.
- Discuss some problems in Korean companies, such as work schedule, drinking, etc.
- What are some problems women have getting a job in Korea? Why?
- How can you find a job?
- Which is more important, your job or your family?
- Would you ever live alone without your husband/wife and children because of your job?

Lesson 05

Pronunciation

Part Ⅰ : /l/ & /r/

Part Ⅱ : /t/

Drills

Part Ⅰ : Q&A – have, need, & want

Q&A – have/want – contrary adjectives

Part Ⅱ : Q&A – What do they do?

Article – Driving and Smartphones Don't Mix

Conversations

Part Ⅰ : Foreign Culture

Part Ⅱ : Travel

Part I

Today's Proverb

"Once bitten, twice shy."

Pronunciation

/l/&/r/: Lip-Rip

A review of /l/ and /r/.

Beginning	Middle	End
lip - rip	be late - berate	appeal - appear
lot - rot	gold- gourd	real - rear
link - rink	pilot - pirate	pole - pour
long - wrong	clop - crop	dial - dire
lock - rock	wild - wired	file - fire
list - wrist	glass - grass	coal - core

1. I'd really like to lock my bicycle to the old birch tree.
2. My Internet connection lost link while uploading a necessary file.
3. I wrote the list on my wrist so I wouldn't forget.
4. A lot of wild berries grow on the hill near my house.
5. In case of fire, you really should dial 119.
6. Barack Obama made a lot of promises to American voters.

Drills

Drill #1: Q&A Drill

(have, need, & want)

Key	Answer
a pencil	*Do you want a pencil?*
(affirmative)	*Thanks, I need a pencil.*
(negative)	*Thanks, but I already have a pencil.*
an eraser	*Do you want an eraser?*
(affirmative)	*Thanks, I need an eraser.*
(negative)	*Thanks, but I already have an eraser.*
1. a comb	Do you want a comb?
2. (affirmative)	Thanks, I need a comb.
3. (negative)	Thanks, but I already have a comb.
4. a handkerchief	Do you want …?
5. (affirmative)	Thanks, I need a …
6. (negative)	Thanks, but I already … handkerchief.
7. a hair band	Do you want …?
8. (affirmative)	Thanks, I need ….
9. (negative)	Thanks, but I already have ….
10. a laptop	… a laptop?
11. (affirmative)	… a laptop.
12. (negative)	… have a laptop.
13. a notebook	… notebook?
14. (affirmative)	…
15. (negative)	Thanks, but ...
16. a battery	…
17. (affirmative)	…
18. (negative)	…
19. a pencil lead	…
20. (affirmative)	…
21. (negative)	…

Drill #2: Q&A Drill

(have/want) – contrary adjectives

Key	Answer
a new pen - have	*Do you have a new pen?* *No, I have an old pen.*
a long skirt - want	*Do you want a long skirt?* *No, I want a short skirt.*
1. a big bag - have	Do you have a …? No, I have a small ….
2. hot tea - want	Do … hot tea? No, … cold …
3. a smart dog - have	Do … dog? … stupid …
4. spicy sauce - want	… spicy …? … mild ...
5. a hard bed - have	…? … soft ...
6. an expensive watch - want	…? …
7. a dull knife - have	…? …
8. a loud voice - have	…? …
9. a tall girlfriend - want	…? …
10. curly hair - have	…? …

Conversations

Conversation: Foreign Culture

1. Do you have any foreign friends?
   a) Yes, I do. I have a friend from the U.S.
   b) No, I don't, but I want to make foreign friends.

2. Where can you meet foreigners in Korea?
   a) There are many foreigners in Itaewon.
   b) Many foreigners live near Haeundae beach in Busan.

3. Which foreign holiday do you like most?
   a) I like Christmas most because I love gifts.
   b) I think Valentine's Day is the most fun.

4. Which country would you like to visit?
   a) I'd like to visit the Czech Republic.
   b) I want to go to New Zealand.

5. What is your opinion of Japan?
   a) I think Japan has great food. I love sushi.
   b) I always worry about Japan's government and army.

6. What is Germany famous for?
   a) German beer is the most famous in the world.
   b) Germany is famous for good car companies.

7. Which country is famous for food?
   a) I think Italy is the most famous country for food in the world.
   b) China is famous for food because you can buy Chinese food in many countries.

8. How do you feel about foreign students in Korea?
   a) I like foreign students. We can have cultural interchange.
   b) I think it is normal. Many Korean students go abroad to study, too.

9. Which city is well-known for shopping in the world?
   a) I think Hong Kong is well-known for shopping.
   b) Paris is well-known for shopping. There are many famous fashion brands in France.

10. Which Korean food is popular among foreigners?
    a) "Bibimbob" is very popular among foreigners.
    b) I think "yookgaejang" is the most popular among foreigners.

11. Do you like western food?
    a) Yes, I do. I like hamburgers and pizza.
    b) No, I don't. I just like Korean food.

12. How often do you watch foreign movies?
    a) I watch Hollywood movies once a month.
    b) I go to the Busan International Film Festival every year and watch several movies.

13. Do you read foreign novels?
    a) Yes, I do. I like classic novels.
    b) No, I don't, but I'd like to read fashion magazines.

14. What image do you have about the Middle East?
    a) I think the Middle East is mysterious.
    b) The Middle East reminds me of a lot of deserts.

15. How can we make foreign friends?
    a) There are many good homepages to find foreign friends.
    b) Applying to work for an international festival, like B.I.F.F., is a good way.

16. Do you like foreign dramas?

17. Which language do you want to study other than English?

18. Where do you want to go for your honeymoon?

19. Which country's people are similar to Koreans?

20. How do foreigners feel about Korea?

Part II

Today's Idiom

"Something came up."

(ex. "I was going to call you yesterday, but something came up.")

Pronunciation

/t/: Toast

To make the /t/ sound, you simply push your tongue to the top of your mouth behind your teeth and, using air to make the sound, drop it quickly. NOTE: A middle /t/ can often make a /d/ sound, especially in American English pronunciation.

Beginning	Middle	End
toast	meeting	advertisement
terrible	little	can't
tiny	city	distribute
tandem	meditation	avert
tea	retailer	sort
tedious	stance	street

1. I ate toast and jam for breakfast.
2. I often talk to the priest when I feel guilty about my mistakes.
3. I did the reading and writing parts in tandem.
4. The little city was at the heart of the country.
5. The retailer decided not to distribute the advertisements on the street.
6. You should avert your eyes when you take a shower with total strangers.

Drills

Drill #1: Q&A Drill

(What do they do?)

Key	Answer
nannies ***babies, take care of***	*What do nannies do?* *They take care of babies.*
1. movie directors **2. movies, make**	What do movie directors do? They make movies.
3. pharmacists **4. medicine, prepare**	What do pharmacists …? They prepare medicine.
5. doctors **6. patients, examine**	What …? …examine patients.
7. architects **8. buildings, construct**	What … do? …construct buildings.
9. veterinarians **10. animals, examine**	What …? They …
11. manufacturers **12. products, manufacture**	…? ...
13. English teachers **14. English, teach**	… …
15. managers **16. affairs, manage**	… …
17. security guards **18. places, guard**	… …
19. flight attendants **20. passengers, serve**	… …

Drill #2: Article

Driving and Smartphones Don't Mix

Marketers are always trying to get consumers to use their company's products as often as possible. Unfortunately, creating a need for a product in a consumer's life can cause situations when the consumer uses the product at inappropriate times.

The smartphone has become notorious for being used at the worst possible times by careless users. In the U.S., more than two-thirds of drivers said that they have used a cell phone while driving at least once in the last month [1].

Drivers Involved in Fatal Crashes by Age and Vehicle Type, 2009

	Total Drivers	Distracted Drivers	Drivers With Cell Phone* (% of Distracted Drivers)
Total	45,230	5,084(11%)	1,006(20%)
Drivers by Age Group			
Under 20	3,967	619(16%)	138(22%)
20-29	10,719	1,378(13%)	293(21%)
30-39	7,633	832(11%)	196(24%)
40-49	7,930	811(10%)	161(20%)
50-59	6,559	631(10%)	124(20%)
60-69	3,968	367(9%)	56(15%)
70+	3,778	408(11%)	37(9%)
Drivers by Vehicte Type			
Passenger Car	18,279	2,044(11%)	386(19%)
Light Truck	17,822	2,117(12%)	475(22%)
Motorcycle	4,593	562(12%)	63(11%)
Large Truck	3,187	257(8%)	75(29%)
Bus	221	14(6%)	3(21%)

Source : NCSA, FARS 2009(ARF)

* The police indicated that the driver was using a cell phlne or a cell phone was in the presence of the driver at the time of the crash.

Making a call, sending a text message, or surfing the web are behaviors that we all do. However, if done while driving a car, they can have disastrous consequences. In a 2006 study, researchers found that the distracting effect of using a cell phone while driving was that of a person with a 0.08 blood-alcohol level, the legal limit for drunk driving in most states [2]. Additionally, it was found that actually holding a cell phone is identical to using hands-free devices when distracting a driver [2]. This means that the conversation with someone on the phone is the factor that distracts and not just holding the device. The unfortunate truth is distraction can lead to death or serious injuries for all people involved, including the driver, passengers, and even pedestrians on the street. In the U.S., fatalities on the road have decreased overall from 2005 through 2009, but the fatalities due to distractions have increased [3]. In South Korea, traffic fatalities ranked 2nd highest of all OECD Countries in 2011, with pedestrian deaths being the highest [4]. One must wonder how many of those cleaths were due to distractions, such as smartphone misuse.

Why do drivers do dangerous and illegal activities such as using a smartphone while driving? Are they aware of the danger they are putting themselves and others in? Drivers are spending more and more time in their cars and want that time to be productive. Rarely do you see people doing just one task these days. Many people are growing accustomed to multitasking in their lives by using their smartphones while watching TV, doing homework, meeting friends, and walking. Unfortunately, multitasking while driving is a game of life and death, and it should not be done. Driving and smartphones don't mix.

Sources:

1. Naumann, R. and Dellinger, A. (2013). Mobile Device Use While Driving — United States and Seven European Countries. *Morbidity and Mortality Weekly Report* (*MMWR*). Center for Disease Control and Prevention. 62 (10); 177-182.

2. Strayer, D. L., Drews, F. A., & Crouch, D. J. (2006). A comparison of the

cell phone driver and the drunk driver. *Human factors: The journal of the human factors and ergonomics society*, 48(2), 381–391.

3. U.S. DOT National Highway Traffic Safety Administration Distacted Drive Report released Sept 2010 http://www-nrd.nhtsa.dot.gov/Pubs/811379.pdf
4. www.oecd.org/statistics/

Comprehension Questions:

1. What do marketers want consumers to do?
2. What percent of drivers in the U.S. have used a cell phone while driving?
3. What is using a cell phone while driving similar to?
4. Is using a hands-free device safer than holding a cell phone while driving?
5. Did fatal accidents on the roads decrease from 2005 to 2009 in the U.S.?
6. Why do drivers use smartphones while driving?
7. According to the table, which age group has the worst percentage of offenders regarding cell phone use in fatal accidents?

Discussion Questions:

1. Do you use your cell phone while driving?
2. Is it illegal in Korea to use smartphones while driving?
3. Is the government restricting your individual rights?
4. Are traffic laws in Korea making you safer on the road?

Conversations

Conversation: Travel

*** Ask partner 1-8, then switch and review. ***

1. Where have you traveled recently?
   a) I took a trip to Jeju last month.
   b) I went to Thailand recently.

2. Who did you go with?
   a) I went there with my friends.
   b) I went there alone.

3. How was the trip?
   a) It was a nice trip. I relaxed a lot.
   b) It rained a lot. I had to stay in the hotel the whole time.

4. How did you travel?
   a) I took a plane from Gimhae airport.
   b) I took a ferry from Busan to Jeju.

5. How much money did you spend for the trip?
   a) I spent only 200,000 won for the trip.
   b) I paid 1,000,000 won for a package trip.

6. What did you do there?
   a) I hiked up Jiri mountain.
   b) I went to the beach and swam a lot.

7. When did you go there?
   a) I went there last weekend.
   b) I went to Jeju last sumnmer.

8. Do you want to go there again?
   a) Yes, I do. It was fun.
   b) No, I don't. I spent too much money there.

9. Do you want to travel this summer vacation?
   a) Yes, I do. I want to go to China this summer vacation.
   b) No, I don't. I have to take some classes during the vacation.

10. Where is the most popular sightseeing place in Korea?
   a) Jeju is the most popular sightseeing place in Korea. It is beautiful there.
   b) I think Gyungju is the best sightseeing place in Korea because of the history.

11. What do you need to pack for traveling?
   a) I need to pack my clothes and cosmetics for traveling.
   b) I need to pack a neck pillow, clothes, and a laptop.

12. When is a good time to travel?
   a) Summer vacation is a great time to travel.
   b) Spring is a good time to travel. It is sunny and cool in spring.

13. Do you like package trips from travel agencies?
   a) Yes, I do. It is easy to follow the schedule from a travel agency.
   b) No, I don't. I want to prepare a travel schedule by myself.

14. Do you like to drive a car when you travel?
   a) Yes, I do. I enjoy driving a car.
   b) No, I don't. I like to use public transportation.

15. Do you usually try traditional foods when you travel?
   a) Yes, I do. I like to eat new foods.
   b) No, I don't. I am afraid of getting sick from new foods.

16. What kind of Korean activities would you recommend to foreigners?

17. Where can you get travel information?

18. What is the most important thing to do when you decide to travel to new places?

19. Where do you usually stay during a trip?

20. Have you ever stayed in a youth hostel?

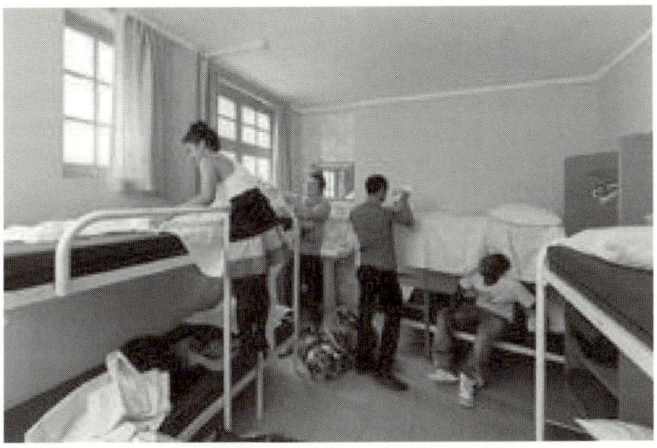

Youth Hostel Van Gogh (Chab) from www.hostels.com

Extra Practice:

- Review some of the previous questions.
- Why do Koreans like foreign brands?
- Where can you buy your favorite foreign brands?
- Why is Korean beef more popular than American beef?

Lesson 06

Pronunciation

Part I : /d/

Part II : /t/ & /d/

Drills

Part I : Substitution – do & ever

Substitution – adverbs of frequency

Part II : Substitution – ever & adverbs of frequency

Article – Satisfying Consumer Needs

Conversations

Part I : Computers

Part II : Free Time

Part I

Today's Proverb

"The darkest hour is just before the dawn."

Pronunciation

/d/: Do

To make the /d/ sound, you simply put the front part of your tongue up against the top of your mouth and, using your voice, drop it quickly.

Beginning	Middle	End
do	sudden	need
doll	modern	barcode
distribute	sandal	sad
dart	abandon	cold
dear	noodles	lid
desire	federal	shed

1. I had a dream about the doll.
2. Dennis doesn't need to practice the drill.
3. Did he deny that he is from Denmark?
4. There is a cold salad under the lid.
5. Damien didn't feel sad, nor did he shed a tear.
6. It's dangerous to eat expired food products.

Drills

Drill #1: Substitution Drill

(do & ever)

Key	Answer
you, study English	*Do you ever study English?*
they	*Do they ever study English?*
he	*Does he ever study English?*

1. go to the gym	Does he ever go to the gym?
2. you	Do you ever ...?
3. listen to the news	Do you ever ...?
4. cook for yourself	... ever cook for yourself?
5. wash dishes	... wash dishes?
6. play the piano	... you ever ...?
7. they	...?
8. ride bicycles	...?
9. read English newspapers	Do they ever ...?
10. buy and sell stocks	Do ...?
11. you	...?
12. he	Does ...?
13. go out to eat	...?
14. go fishing	...?
15. watch CNN	...?
16. go camping	...?
17. she	...?
18. they	...?
19. call their friends	Do they ...?
20. write letters	Do they ever write letters?

Drill #2: Substitution Drill

(adverbs of frequency)

Key	Answer
always, go to E-mart	*I always go to E-mart.*
hardly ever	*I hardly ever go to E-mart.*
nervous	*I'm hardly ever nervous.*
1. usually	I'm usually nervous.
2. watch CNN	I usually watch CNN.
3. often	I often ...
4. he	... watches ...
5. practice English pronunciation	He ... practices ...
6. never	He never ...
7. they	They never practice ....
8. sometimes	They sometimes ...
9. play baseball	They ...
10. always	...
11. rarely	...
12. tired	... rarely tired.
13. she	She is ...
14. do yoga	She ... does ...
15. seldom	... seldom ...
16. hardly ever	...
17. I	... hardly ever ...
18. cheerful	I am ...
19. often	I am often cheerful.
20. usually	...

Conversations

Conversation: Computers

1. Do you have your own computer?
   a) Yes, I do. I have my own laptop.
   b) No, I don't, but I want to buy a computer soon.

2. Have you heard of a Netbook?
   a) Yes, I have. It is smaller than a laptop.
   b) No, I haven't. I don't know what it is.

Samsung NC110 Netbook

3. What do you use a computer for?
   a) I check my email and watch the stock market.
   b) I play computer games and chat with my friends.

4. When did you use a computer first?
   a) I first used a computer in middle school for homework.
   b) I first learned to use a computer when I was 9 years old.

5. Which company is famous for computers?
   a) Dell is famous for computers in the world.
   b) Samsung is famous for computers in Korea.

6. Where is a good place to buy a computer?
   a) Himart is a good place to buy a computer because it has good prices.
   b) Internet shopping malls are cheaper than other computer stores.

7. Which company's Internet service do you use?
   a) I use LG's Internet service. It's very fast.
   b) I use an Internet service called SK Broadband.

8. Are you interested in studying computer languages?
   a) Yes, I am. I'd like to study JAVA.
   b) No, I'm not. I don't think they are necessary to use computers.

9. Which software program do you use for editing documents?
   a) I use Hangul Word Processor for editing documents. It's great for Korean text.
   b) I use MS Word for editing documents. It is best for typing in English.

10. Do you have any antivirus programs on your computer?
   a) Yes, I do. I have an antivirus programs on my computer called "Avira."
   b) No, I don't, but I want to get one soon.

11. How much time do you spend using a computer?
   a) I use a computer for 2 hours a day.
   b) I use a computer for less than 30 minutes a day.

12. Do you listen to music through your computer?
   a) Yes, I do. My computer has good speakers.
   b) No, I don't. I usually use my smartphone for listening to music.

13. How old is your computer?
   a) It is 3 years old.
   b) I bought a new computer last month.

14. What brand of computer do you have?
    a) It is a Samsung. I really like it.
    b) It is an LG. I just bought it.

15. Do you have any computer certificates?
    a) Yes, I do. I have a certificate for word processing.
    b) No, I don't, but I want to get one for MS Excel.

16. Do you like computer games?

17. Who fixes your computer when it is broken?

18. Do you ever download music on the Internet?

19. Do you ever chat with your friends on the Internet?

20. Do you have your own homepage? (e.g. Facebook or Cyworld)

6

Part Ⅱ

Today's Idiom

"... in the dead of night."

(ex. "Johnnie called me in the dead of night.")

Pronunciation

/t/&/d/: Time - Dime

A review of /d/ and /t/ through minimal pairing.

Beginning	Middle	End
time - dime	sighting - siding	pat - pad
tore - door	whiter - wider	sat - sad
team - deem	hurting - herding	bite - bide
train - drain	liter - leader	wait - wade
two - do	waiting - wading	clout - cloud
tip - dip	center - sender	height - hide

1. Tim took his time deciding what to do.
2. Two heads are better than one.
3. Ten liters of water isn't enough to cross the desert.
4. You should leave a 15% tip for your waiter at the diner.
5. He knocked at the door, and I hid under the bed.
6. My pet cat ate her food but didn't drink the water.

Drills

Drill #1: Q&A Drill

("ever" and adverbs of frequency)

Key	Answer
you - depressed ***often***	*Are you ever depressed?* *Yes, I'm often depressed.*
Henry - read books ***always***	*Does Henry ever read books?* *Yes, he always reads books.*

1. you - tired **always**	Are you ever tired? Yes, I'm always tired.
2. Susan - wear contact lenses **often**	Does Susan ever ...? Yes, she often wears ...
3. you - lonely **often**	Are you ever ...? Yes, I'm ...
4. Tom - clean his room **always**	Does Tom ...? Yes, he always ...
5. you - nervous **always**	Are ...? Yes, I'm ...
6. Kelly - call her friends **often**	Does ...? Yes, she ...
7. Lori - happy **often**	..? ...
8. you - go skating **always**	..? ...
9. Jennifer - angry **often**	..? ...
10. you - play the piano **always**	..? ...

Drill #2: Article

Satisfying Consumer Needs – The Four Ps: Controllable Marketing Mix Factors

(Kerin, Hartley, Berkowitz, and Rudelius. Marketing 8th ed., NY:McGraw-Hill/Irwin, 2006. pg14.)

Vocabulary Words

satisfy, discovery, organization, concentrate, efforts, specific, potential, consumers, to direct, target market, to take action, develop, shorthand, reference.

"Satisfying Consumer Needs

Marketing doesn't stop with the discovery of consumer needs. Because the organization obviously can't satisfy all consumer needs, it must concentrate its efforts on certain needs of a specific group of potential consumers. This is the target market---one or more specific groups of potential consumers toward which an organization directs its marketing program."

"The Four Ps: Controllable Marketing Mix Factors

Having selected the target market consumers, the firm must take steps to satisfy their needs. Someone in the organization's marketing department, often the marketing manager, must take action and develop a complete marketing program to reach consumers by using a combination of four tools, often called the four Ps---a useful shorthand reference to them first published by Professor E. Jerome McCarthy:

- Product. A good, service, or idea to satisfy the consumer's needs.
- Price. What is exchanged for the product.
- Promotion. A means of communication between the seller and buyer.
- Place. A means of getting the product into the consumer's hands.

…These are the marketing manager's controllable factors---product, price, promotion, and place———that can be used to solve a marketing problem."

Comprehension Questions:

1. Can an organization satisfy all consumer needs?
2. What is the shorthand version of the tool used by marketing managers?
3. What are the four Ps?
4. What does each 'P' mean exactly?
5. What factors can marketing managers control?

Discussion Questions:

1. Have you heard of the four Ps before reading this article?
2. Which of the four Ps is important to you for most purchases?
3. Do you think a marketing manager's job is difficult? Why or why not?
4. What kind of promotions are common in Korea?
5. Where is the best place to open a Nike shoe store in this city?
6. What products or services do you usually buy?

Conversations

Conversation: Free Time

1. What do you do when you have free time?
   a) I read books when I have free time.
   b) I watch TV when I'm free.

2. Do you like to go to the theater?
   a) Yes, I do. I like to see movies in the theater.
   b) No, I don't. I like to watch movies at home.

3. What kinds of movies do you like?
   a) I like horror movies, like Saw.
   b) I prefer watching action flicks, like Terminator.

4. Do you like reading books?
   a) Yes, I do. I read books everyday.
   b) No, I don't. I don't enjoy reading books at all.

5. Do you read newspapers regularly?
   a) Yes, I often read the Korean Herald.
   b) No, I don't. I just browse the news on the Internet.

The Korea Herald ENGLISH EDITION

National | Business | Life & Style | Entertainment | Sports | World | Opinion

SUBSCRIBE PDF SMS/LMS MOBILE APP NEST

Lack of drone defense raises ire

Criticism is mounting over the South Korean military's ill-preparedness against North Korea's drone-based military act...

Further punishment possible over N. Kore...
Chinese media tells N. Korea to 'abandon...
Samsung pushes for major restructuring

Obama may visit Seoul on April 25

U.S. President Barack Obama is expected to visit South Korea on April 25 following a three-day ...

USFK chief warns of N.K. surprise attack, fallout from budget cuts

WASHINGTON (Yonhap) — The North Korean regime is so dangerous that it can attack South Korea w...

Samsung, Google and homosexuality

Perhaps it is not surprising that a gap exists between Silicon Valley IT firms such as Google a...

6. Have you ever watched English movies without a translation?
   a) Yes, I have. I watched Shrek without a translation.
   b) No, I haven't. I will try it someday.

7. Do you like to play musical instruments?
   a) Yes, I do. I like to play the piano.
   b) No, I don't. I prefer to listen to music.

8. What musical instrument can you play?
   a) I can play the piano. I have played for 2 years.
   b) I can't play any instruments, but I enjoy singing.

9. What do you do when you are home alone?
   a) I watch TV when I'm home alone.
   b) I listen to music.

10. Do you like to cook?
   a) Yes, I do. I like cooking Korean food.
   b) No, I don't. I'm not good at cooking.

11. Do you like being alone?
   a) Yes, I do. I can think about my life when I'm alone.
   b) No, I don't. I can be bored easily when I'm alone.

12. What do you want to do if you have a week free?
   a) I want to stay home and do nothing.
   b) I want to read comic books for a whole week.

13. Do you exercise regularly?
   a) Yes, I do. I do yoga everyday.
   b) No, I don't. I think I'm lazy.

14. Do you think you are busy?
    a) Yes, I do. I have to study and work.
    b) No, I don't. I have a lot of free time in the afternoon.

15. Do you think that you manage your time well?
    a) Yes, I do. I check my schedule every morning.
    b) No, I don't. I think I need to plan my time better than now.

16. Who do you spend your time with the most?

17. Where do you spend the majority of your time?

18. When do you think that you are wasting your time?

19. How much time do you spend studying?

20. Do you wish you had more free time?

Extra Practice:

- Review some of the previous questions.
- What can you do if your computer won't print your paper?
- Do you trust LG's after-sales service? How about Samsung's?
- How do you spend your weekends?
- What do guys and girls do differently during their free time?
- How should we use free time at our jobs?

Lesson 07

Pronunciation

Part I : /t/, /d/, /id/ : -ed (regular past)

Part II : /Θ/, or /th/

Drills

Part I : Substitution – pronouns + with
Article – Goals

Part II : Q&A – pronouns + with
Article – A Memo from the Boss

Conversations

Part I : Friends and Parties

Part II : Introducing Korean Culture

Part I

Today's Proverb

"There's no such thing as a free lunch."

Pronunciation

/t/, /d/, /id/: -ed

When you have an -ed ending to a verb, it can make one of three distinct sounds:

- A voiceless ending + -ed will usually make a /t/ sound.
- A voiced ending + -ed will usually make a /d/ sound.
- A /t/ or /d/ ending + -ed will usually make an /id/ sound to make the past tense clear.

-/t/	-/d/	-/id/
walked	learned	wanted
jumped	cried	pointed
laughed	spammed	needed
washed	loved	aided
watched	stayed	started
helped	dreamed	united

1. I have always hoped that North and South Korea will be reunited.
2. Samsung manufactured products, distributed advertisements, and helped customers.
3. I watched two Hyundai cars being produced yesterday.
4. I've always hated getting spammed with junk emails.
5. He killed two birds with one stone.
6. Heather always dreamed about things she wanted.

Drills

Drill #1: Substitution Drill

(pronouns + "with")

Key	Answer
I have my pens with me.	*I have my pens with me.*
she	*She has her pens with her.*
(question)	*Does she have her pens with her?*
1. he	Does he have his pens … him?
2. headphones	Does he have … headphones with …?
3. (statement)	… has … headphones with ...
4. you	You … headphones with ...
5. (negative)	You don't ...
6. Jenny	Jenny doesn't have her …
7. (affirmative)	Jenny has ….
8. they	They ...
9. money	… their money …
10. I	I … me.
11. (question)	Do … me?
12. she	Does …?
13. (statement)	She ...
14. Mike and I	Mike and I …
15. the kids	… them.
16. (negative)	...
17. their cat	... their cat with …
18. Jennifer	...
19. he	...
20. (affirmative)	...

Drill #2: Article

Goals

(Kerin, Hartley, Berkowitz, and Rudelius. Marketing 8th ed., NY: McGraw-Hill/Irwin, 2006. Pg34.)

Vocabulary Words

ROI (Return on Investment), to elect, maximize, maintain, at the expense of, status, prestige, to be at stake, ratio, revenue, perceptions, vital, explicit, to state, commitment, working conditions, welfare

"Business firms can pursue several different types of goals:

Profit : Classic economic theory assumes a firm seeks to get as high a financial return on its investment---profit---as possible.

Sales : If profits are acceptable, a firm may elect to maintain or increase its sales level even though profitability may not be maximized.

Market share : A firm may choose to maintain or increase its market share, sometimes at the expense of greater profits if industry status or prestige is at stake. Market share is the ratio of sales revenue of the firm to the total sales revenue of all firms in the industry, including the firm itself.

Quality : A firm may target the highest quality...

Customer satisfaction : Customers are the reason the organization exists, so their perceptions and actions are of vital importance.

Employee welfare : A firm may recognize the critical importance of its employees by having an explicit goal stating its commitment to good employment opportunities and working conditions for them.

Social responsibility : A firm may seek to balance conflicting goals of consumers, employees, and stockholders to promote overall welfare of all these groups, even at the expense of profits."

Comprehension Questions:

1. What are the different goals that a business firm can try to accomplish?
2. Can you explain what a "market share" is?
3. What is "customer satisfaction"?
4. How can a firm focus on employee welfare?
5. Who is important when a firm tries to focus on social responsibility?

Discussion Questions:

1. If you could work for a company with one of the goals from the list, what company would you like to work for?
2. What do most companies in Korea have as their primary goals?
3. What kinds of things do companies do that focus on social responsibility?
4. Why do many companies think that profit is their main goal?

Conversations

Conversation: Friends and Parties

1. Do you like parties?
   a) Yes, I do. I often have parties with my friends.
   b) No, I don't. I don't like to go to parties.

2. What kind of party do you like?
   a) I love my birthday party every year.
   b) I don't like any parties.

3. Do you like surprise parties?
   a) Yes, I like them. They are always fun.
   b) I don't know. I've never been to a surprise party.

4. What kind of party do you want to try with your friends?
   a) I want to try a pajama party with my friends.
   b) A graduation party would be fun.

5. Which party did you recently go to?
   a) I went to a Christmas party in my church.
   b) I recently attended my sister's baby shower.

6. Where is a good place to hold a small party?
   a) Pizza restaurants are great places to hold a small party with friends.
   b) I think buffet restaurants are good.

7. Do you like to drink during a party?
   a) Yes, I do. I think soju is best for a party.
   b) No, I don't. I don't like drinking.

8. What will you do for your next birthday?
   a) I will invite my friends to my house.
   b) I will go to a bar with my friends and have a small party there.

9. What do you usually buy for your friend's birthday present?
   a) I usually buy cosmetics for my friends.
   b) I just buy a birthday cake.

10. What was the best birthday gift you have ever received?
    a) A laptop computer was the best gift that I've received. My father gave it to me.
    b) Money is the best gift that I've gotten. My grandfather gave me 100,000 won.

11. How do you spend Valentine's Day?
    a) I usually go to a nice restaurant with my girlfriend/boyfriend.
    b) I don't do anything special.

12. Does your family enjoy having a party?
    a) Yes, we do. We always try to celebrate special days.
    b) No, we don't because my family lives in other cities.

13. What do you do on Parents' Day?
    a) I buy red carnations for my parents.
    b) I write letters to my parents.

14. What do you do with your friends on the weekends?
    a) We go to a nightclub and dance a lot.
    b) I don't get together with my friends on the weekends.

15. Who is your best friend? Where did you meet him/her?
    a) My best friend is Jihyun. I met her in elementary school.
    b) Jungho is my best friend. I met him at my previous job.

16. How many good friends do you have?

17. Can a man and a woman be friends?

18. What do you usually do on Christmas Day?

19. Where do you usually buy gifts for your friends?

20. Have you ever bought a gift from an Internet shopping mall?

7

Part Ⅱ

Today's Proverb

"... get it over with."

(ex. "Let's just get this test over with.")

Pronunciation

/θ/, or /th/: Think

To make the /θ/ sound, you simply put your tongue between your teeth and blow out air, but don't bite down on your tongue.

Beginning	Middle	End
thing	birthday	faith
thick	something	teeth
thirst	ethical	path
theater	athlete	worth
thousand	healthy	oath
throat	within	growth

1. He went to the theater on Thursday.
2. Three thousand people went to see the athlete.
3. I feel like I have something in my teeth.
4. I keep clearing my throat, so maybe I'm unhealthy.
5. The path to heaven begins with a strong faith.
6. It is unethical to break an oath with someone.

Drills

Drill #1: Q&A Drill

(pronouns + "with")

Key	Answer
use, your book	*Can I use your book?* *I don't have my book with me.*
where, your watch	*Where is your watch?* *I don't have my watch with me.*

1. use - your brush	Can I use your …? I don't have my … with me.
2. where - her running shoes	Where are her …? She doesn't have her … with her.
3. use - his umbrella	Can I … umbrella? He … his umbrella with him.
4. where - your cell phone	Where is …? I … my … with me.
5. use - their backpack	Can I …? They … their … them.
6. where - our MP3 player	… our …? We … our MP3 player … us.
7. use - your jacket	Can I …? I don't … with ...
8. where - her scarf	Where …? She … her.
9. use - their camera	...? ...
10. where – his laptop	...? ...

Drill #2: Article

A Memo from the Boss

To: All staff

From: Heather Snow

Date: June 25th

Subject: Independence Day

As you know, Independence Day is just around the corner. There will be no work on Independence Day and the day after Independence Day, so you don't have to come in on those days. I want you to finish all of your tasks by 5pm on the Friday before. If you do not finish your work, then don't worry about it. Please go home and enjoy the time with your family and children.

I will be busy with my family during the holiday. Please do not call me because I will not answer my phone. If you need to contact me, send an email. I will read the email and reply when I have time.

Remember that next Friday is the special office day, "Green Friday", so if you wear any green clothes, I will buy you a coffee from Starbucks.

Questions

1. What holiday is coming?
2. What days will there be no work?
3. When should you finish all of your tasks?
4. What should you do if you don't finish your tasks by then?
5. Can you call Ms. Snow during the break?
6. How can you contact Ms. Snow during the break?
7. What is special about next Friday?
8. Is next Friday a holiday?

Extra: What does "just around the corner" mean?

Conversations

Conversation: Introducing Korean Culture

1. What is your favorite part of Korean culture?
   a) I love Korean pop music.
   b) I really enjoy eating Korean food.

2. What do you think about Korean movies?
   a) I think Korean movies are better than Hollywood movies.
   b) Korean movies have very good stories. They are interesting.

3. What mountain have you hiked up recently?
   a) I haven't gone hiking lately.
   b) I hiked up Jang Mountain last weekend.

4. Have you read any Korean novels lately?
   a) Yes, I have. I read a novel set during the Korean Civil War.
   b) No, I haven't. I don't have time to read these days.

5. Which Korean newspaper do you read?
   a) I usually read the Joong-ang newspaper.
   b) I don't read newspapers. I just read the news online.

6. Which place in Korea do you want to visit?
   a) I really want to go to Jeju in the summer. It's so beautiful.
   b) I want to go to Seoul to go shopping. There are more markets there.

7. Where can a tourist buy some souvenirs?
   a) Nampodong is a good place for tourists to shop.
   b) Tourists should go to Beomeosa Temple to buy some souvenirs.

8. What musical instruments are famous in Korea?

   a) Many Koreans play the piano.

   b) I think the Korean drums are the most famous in Korea.

9. Do you own a "Hanbok"?

   a) Yes, I do. I have a "hanbok" in my apartment.

   b) No I don't. People don't wear "hanboks" these days.

10. What do you do during Chuseok?

   a) I usually spend Chuseok with my family at home.

   b) My family goes to the mountain to bow to our ancestors' graves.

11. What is your favorite Korean holiday?

   a) I really love Buddha's Birthday. The temple lights are so pretty at night.

   b) I think Chuseok is my favorite Korean holiday.

12. What do you think the best Korean food is?

   a) Kimchi is the best Korean food because it's so healthy.

   b) Bulgogi is the best food because it is so delicious.

13. When will North and South Korea reunify?

   a) I don't know, but I think we will reunify soon.

   b) I think we will reunify within 50 years.

14. Do you think that Korea is a great place to live?
    a) Yes, I do. I love Korea, and I think it is beautiful.
    b) No, I don't. It's too crowded, and the economy isn't good.

15. Where can you go to learn about Korean history?
    a) You should go to Gyungju to learn about Korean history.
    b) There are many good museums in Busan.

16. Where do you want to live when you are 40 years old?

17. What are some famous Korean traditional songs?

18. Where is the most beautiful place in Korea?

19. Do you want to go sightseeing in North Korea?

20. Why are North and South Korean cultures different?

Extra Practice:

- Review some of the previous questions.
- Tell about the "Membership Training"* program you went to.
- Have you ever been to a party with your professor? When?
- What age is the most fun to be? Why do you think so?
- What do you think of group dating or blind dates?
- What makes Koreans unique?
- Why is learning Chinese characters useful?

* "membership training" is "school retreat" in Correct English. (See Lesson 13.)

Lesson 08

Pronunciation

Part Ⅰ : /ð/or /thz/

Part Ⅱ : /Θ/ & /ð/

Drills

Part Ⅰ : Substitution – majors

Q&A – "Where can you buy..." & one/some

Article – BBC.com – Bad Bosses Can Damage Your Heart

Part Ⅱ : Q&A – contrary adjectives

Substitution – past tense of "be"

Conversations

Part Ⅰ : Stress

Part Ⅱ : Love and Dating

Part I

Today's Proverb

"You can lead a horse to water, but you can't make it drink."

Pronunciation

/ð/ or /thz/: They

To make the /ð/ sound, just put your tongue between your teeth and use your voice.

Beginning	Middle	End
they	bother	mouth
their	leather	breathe
then	either	teethe
the	weather	smooth
there	mother	soothe
that	gather	bathe

1. My mother soothes my heart when I'm either sad or lonely.
2. This, that, these, or those are all good.
3. If you want to bother me, why don't you go over there?
4. This leather is gathered and shipped from many other places.
5. When it's hot and humid, the weather makes it difficult to breathe.
6. The Catholics often call the priests "Father."

Drills

Drill #1: Substitution Drill

(major)

Key	Answer
I, English	*I'm majoring in English*
she	*She's majoring in English.*

Key	Answer
1. he	He's majoring in English.
2. architecture	He's majoring in architecture.
3. they	They're … in architecture.
4. you	You're … in architecture.
5. economics	You're majoring ...
6. I	I'm majoring ...
7. she	… in economics.
8. music	… in music.
9. engineering	She's … engineering.
10. education	She's … education.
11. they	… education.
12. Chinese	… Chinese.
13. philosophy	They're ...
14. I	I'm ...
15. physics	...
16. trade	...
17. she	...
18. archaeology	...
19. he	… in archaeology.
20. accounting	He's …

Drill #2: Q&A Drill

("Where can you buy...") with ("one" and "some")

Key	Answer
Where, pencils *a stationary store*	*Where can you buy pencils?* *You can buy some in a stationary store.*
1. where, a computer	Where can you buy a computer?
2. a computer store	You can buy one in a computer store.
3. where, a scarf	Where can you buy a scarf?
4. a clothing store	You can buy one in a clothing store.
5. where, earrings	… buy earrings?
6. a jewelry store	… some in a jewelry store.
7. where, snacks	… buy snacks?
8. a grocery store	… some in a grocery store.
9. where, ice cream	Where can you …?
10. an ice cream parlor	You can buy some ...
11. where, lotion	Where … lotion?
12. a cosmetics store	… some in a ...
13. where, CDs	Where … CDs?
14. a music store	You … some ...
15. where, books	… buy books?
16. a bookstore	… some ...
17. where, MP3s	… MP3s?
18. online	… online.
19. where, a bicycle	… a …?
20. a bike shop	… one ...

Drill #3: Article

BBC.com – Bad Bosses Can Damage Your Heart

(Nov 25, 2008 http://news.bbc.co.uk/2/hi/7745324.stm)

Inconsiderate bosses not only make work stressful, they may also increase the risk of heart disease for their employees, experts believe.

A Swedish team found a strong link between poor leadership and the risk of serious heart disease and heart attacks among more than 3,000 employed men. And the effect may be cumulative – the risk went up the longer an employee worked for the same company.

The study is published in Occupational and Environmental Medicine.

Feeling undervalued can use stress

Stressful environment

Experts said that feeling undervalued and unsupported at work can cause stress, which often fosters unhealthy behaviours, such as smoking, that can lead to heart disease.

Previous work has shown that unfair bosses can drive up their employees' blood pressure, and persistent high blood pressure can increase heart disease risk. For the latest study, researchers from the Karolinska Institute and Stockholm University tracked the heart health of the male employees, aged between 19 and 70 and working in the Stockholm area, over a period of nearly a decade. During this time 74 cases of fatal and non–fatal heart attack or [chest pain], or death from ··· heart disease, occurred.

All the participants were asked to rate the leadership style of their senior managers on competencies such as how clearly they set out goals for their staff and how good they were at communicating and giving feedback.

The staff who deemed their senior managers to be the least competent had a 25% higher risk of a serious heart problem. And those working for what was classed as a long time – four years or more – had a 64% higher risk.

"Feeling undervalued and unsupported can cause stress, which often leads to unhealthy behaviours ... adding to your risk of developing heart problems."

-Cathy Ross of the British Heart Foundation

The findings held true, regardless of educational attainment, social class, income, workload, lifestyle factors, such as smoking and exercise, and other risk factors for heart disease, such as high blood pressure and diabetes.

The researchers, which included experts from University College London in the UK and the Finnish Institute of Occupational Health, said that if a direct cause and effect was confirmed, then managers' behaviour should be targeted [to reduce] serious heart disease among less senior employees. They said managers should give employees clear work objectives and sufficient power in relation to their responsibilities.

Cathy Ross, cardiac nurse for the British Heart Foundation, said: "This limited, male-only study suggests that a good, clear working relationship with your manager may help to protect against heart disease. ... Feeling undervalued and unsupported can cause stress, which often leads to unhealthy behaviours such as smoking, eating a poor diet, drinking too much alcohol and not getting enough exercise – adding to your risk of developing heart problems. ... Being fit and active can give you the double benefit of [reducing] work stress and [improving] your heart health at the same time.

Conversations

Conversation: Stress

1. What is stress?
    a) Stress is when you are too worried about something.
    b) I think stress is when you are unhappy.

2. What causes stress in your life?
    a) My parents cause me stress because they are too strict.
    b) Finding a job is very stressful for me.

3. How do you like to relax?
   a) I like to sleep to relax, so I nap often.
   b) I like to spend time with my friends to relax.

4. What was your most stressful test recently?
   a) This class's mid–term test was the most stressful test so far.
   b) My marketing class had a really stressful test recently.

5. Are you feeling stressed these days?
   a) Yes I am, I'm very stressed these days. I am so busy.
   b) No, I'm not. I don't feel stressed these days. I have a lot of free time.

6. What do you do when you are really angry?
   a) When I am angry, I like to go to a karaoke room and sing.
   b) I always talk to my mother when I am really angry about something.

7. Are you really busy these days?
   a) No, I'm not that busy these days. I don't get much homework.
   b) Yes, I am busy studying for my classes.

8. Do you want to work hard or have an easy job?
   a) I want to work hard and make a lot of money.
   b) I want an easy job, so I can be happy and enjoy my life.

9. Do you like to be busy?
   a) Yes, I do. I like being busy. It makes time pass quickly.
   b) Sometimes, I do. However, if I am too busy, I am not happy.

10. Do you ever listen to music when you are stressed?
   a) Yes, my favorite kind of music to listen to when I am stressed is jazz.
   b) No, I don't. I usually like to go to sleep.

11. Is drinking alcohol a good way to reduce stress?
    a) Yes, it is. Many Koreans drink alcohol to reduce stress.
    b) No it isn't. After drinking, the problems still exist, and I just have a hang-over.

12. Do you think smoking causes more stress or reduces stress?
    a) I know that smoking causes more stress because you always need another cigarette to relax.
    b) Whenever I smoke, I feel relaxed, so smoking helps me.

13. What is the most stressful job you can think of?
    a) I think being a soldier is the most stressful job because the army is so strict.
    b) People really hate being a nurse in Korea because it is so stressful.

14. Are you happy these days?
    a) Yes, I am. I am very happy these days. My life is great!
    b) No, I'm not. I feel blue these days.

15. Which is more stressful; dating or being single?
    a) Dating is more stressful. My girlfriend drives me crazy.
    b) I hate being single. I always worry about who I will marry.

16. Tell me about a stressful situation you experienced.

17. Who makes you feel the most stress in your daily life?

18. Which class is the most stressful for you this term?

19. Which class is the least stressful for you this term?

20. Tell me about some ways to get rid of stress.

Part II

Today's Proverb

"... to hit rock bottom."

(ex. "When Julia left him, he hit rock bottom.")

Pronunciation

/θ/ & /ð/: Think-Them

This is a review of /θ/ and /ð/through the use of minimal pairs.

Beginning	Middle	End
thigh - thy	ether - either	mouth - mouth
-	-	wreath - wreathe
-	-	sheath - sheathe
-	-	teeth - teethe

1. The thing over there is either everything or nothing.
2. Which month do you think that his mother would rather sun bathe?
3. The northern and southern parts of North America have different weather systems.
4. Throughout his life, he always thought about the death of his brother.
5. They are always worried about their health.
6. Babies get new teeth in their mouths when they teethe.

8

Drills

Drill #1: Q&A Drill

(contrary adjectives)

Key	Answer
read an old book	*Did you read an old book?* *No, it was a new book.*

Key	Answer
1. buy an expensive watch **2.**	Did you buy an expensive watch? No, it was a cheap watch.
3. turn on a bright light **4.**	Did you turn on a bright light? No, it was a dim light
5. use a sharp pencil **6.**	… you use a sharp pencil? … was a dull pencil.
7. wear long socks **8.**	Did you … socks No, … short...
9. drink cold tea **10.**	… cold tea? No, it … hot ...
11. take a difficult class **12.**	… difficult …? … an easy …
13. bring a thick book **14.**	… …
15. sit on a clean chair **16.**	… …
17. wear a wet sweater **18.**	… …
19. watch a fun movie **20.**	… …

Drill #2: Substitution Drill

(past tense of "be")

Key	Answer
I, annoyed	*I was annoyed.*
we	*We were annoyed.*
1. the kids	The kids were annoyed.
2. confused	The kids … confused.
3. (negative)	The kids weren't ….
4. he	He wasn't ….
5. worried	He ….
6. you	… weren't ...
7. (affirmative)	…were ...
8. fascinated	...
9. she	She ….
10. I	....
11. (question)	Was …?
12. invited	Was I …?
13. they	…?
14. (statement)	…were invited.
15. relaxed	...
16. Mike	Mike was ...
17. excited	...
18. we	....
19. interested	…were ...
20. he	…

Conversations

Conversation: Love and Dating

1. Do you have a boyfriend/girlfriend?
   a) Yes, I do. I have a girlfriend. Her name is Ji—yoon
   b) No, I don't. I'm single. I like being alone.

2. Have you ever been on a blind date?
   a) Yes, I have. I have been on a blind date two times.
   b) No, I haven't. I don't like to go on a date with a stranger.

3. Where is a good place to go on a date?
   a) I like to go to a bar and drink on a date. We can relax and talk freely.
   b) The best place to go on a date is the beach. It's very romantic.

4. Are any of your friends married?
   a) Yes, they are. Two of my friends are married.
   b) No, they aren't. None of my friends are married yet.

5. What is the best gift to receive from your girlfriend/boyfriend?
   a) I hope my boyfriend gives me a promise ring. That is the best gift.
   b) I love to get chocolate from my boyfriend. I love chocolate.

6. When do you want to get married?
   a) I want to get married before I'm 30 years old.
   b) I don't want to get married. I want to focus on my career.

7. Where can you meet a good person to date?
   a) I think the night club is the best place to meet good people.
   b) Church is the best place to meet a good person.

8. Who should pay for dinner; the man, the woman, or should they "go Dutch"?
   a) Going Dutch is the best way. Everybody can pay for their own food.
   b) I think the man should pay for the food. That is the traditional way.

9. Would you rather marry a rich, ugly person or a good-looking, poor person?
   a) I'm not sure, I think I want to marry a normal-looking, middle class person.
   b) I want to marry a good-looking girl. I don't care if she is poor.

10. When do you want to have children? How many do you want to have?
   a) I don't want to have children. Education is too expensive.
   b) I want to have children before I am 35 years old. I want to have 3; a son and two daughters.

11. Have you ever loved someone, but they didn't love you?
   a) Yes, I have. I loved one girl in high school, but she didn't notice me.
   b) Sorry, but I can't remember.

12. Where did your parents first meet?
   a) My parents met each other in high school.
   b) My parents met on a blind date.

13. What is something you really hate when you are dating?
   a) I really hate it when my date smokes. It really smells bad.
   b) I really hate it when we don't have enough money to do something fun.

14. Is it ok for co-workers to date each other?
   a) No, it isn't. Dating a co-worker is bad because breaking up makes a lot of problems for the staff.
   b) Yes, it is. I think it's ok to date someone you like in your company.

15. Where do you want to go on your honeymoon?

16. What is the perfect date?

17. What is your ideal type?

18. Would you like to date a famous person? If so, who?

19. What are the best clothes to wear on a first date?

20. If your parents hated your boyfriend/girlfriend, what would you do?

Scene from the movie "Love Actually"

Extra Practice:

- Review the previous questions with your group, or ask new questions.
- What will you do after you graduate? Where will you go? What job do you want?
- What are some of the most stressful problems in a job?
- What are some of the most stressful problems in a relationship?
- What is your ideal life?
- Why do people break up?

Lesson 09

Pronunciation

Part Ⅰ : /s/

Part Ⅱ : /z/

Drills

Part Ⅰ : Q&A – contrary adjectives

Q&A – singular general and specific pronouns

Part Ⅱ : Q&A – plural general and specific pronouns

Sentence Transformation – present progressive → past tense

Article – The Characteristics of High Self - Confidence

Conversations

Part Ⅰ : Music

Part Ⅱ : Health

9

Part I

Today's Proverb

"What doesn't kill you, makes you stronger."

Pronunciation

/s/: Self

To make the /s/ sound, you have to put your tongue behind your teeth and let just a little air pass over the tip of your tongue. Koreans usually make the /s/ sound too deep in their mouths.

Beginning	Middle	End
self-esteem	customer	access
search	aspect	experience
selling	essay	place
service	consumer	products
synergy	assume	price
sales	basic	address

1. I got seasick when I was on the boat after supper on Saturday.
2. The customer likes to shop at Save Zone for Christmas.
3. I assume you already did the basic job assignments.
4. I do not have the password to access the computer system.
5. A company and its salespeople can have a synergy effect together for a customer.
6. Sam took a selfie with his smartphone stick.

Drills

Drill #1: Q&A Drill

(contrary adjectives)

Key	Answer
The book - interesting	*Was the book interesting?* *No, it was boring.*
the dogs - big	*Were the dogs big?* *No, they were small.*

Key	Answer
1. the room - clean **2.**	Was the room ...? No, it was ...
3. the vegetables - fresh **4.**	Were the vegetables ...? No, they ... rotten.
5. the music - loud **6.**	Was the music loud? ... was quiet.
7. the models - tall **8.**	Were ... models ...? No, they ...
9. the mid-term test - easy **10.**	... mid-term test ...? ... difficult.
11. the plans - practical **12.**	...? ... impractical.
13. the answer - clear **14.**	...? ... confusing.
15. the oranges - sweet **16.**	...? ... sour.
17. the teacher - easygoing **18.**	...? ...
19. the athletes - out of shape **20.**	...? ... in shape.

Drill #2: Q&A Drill

Pronoun Use

	General (e.g. a computer)	Specific (e.g. the computer)
Singular (e.g. a / the dog)	One	It
Plural (e.g. dogs / the dogs)	(affirmative) Some (negative) Any	Them
Uncountable (e.g. water / the water)	(affirmative) Some (negative) Any	It

(singular general and specific pronouns – one/it)

Key	Answer
Sing - a song ***Yes***	*Did you sing a song?* *Yes, I sang one.*
Play - the piano ***No***	*Did you play the piano?* *No, I didn't play it.*

1. have - an eraser **2. yes**	Did you have an eraser? Yes, ... had one.
3. wear - the scarf **4. no**	Did you wear ...? No, I ... wear it.
5. take - a test **6. yes**	... take a test? Yes, ... one.
7. write - the card **8. no**	Did ... the card? No, ... it.
9. eat - an ice cream cone **10. yes**	Did ... eat an ice cream cone? ... one.
11. use - the lotion **12. no**	... the lotion? ... it.
13. take - a bath **14. no**	...? ...

15. drink - the milk	...?
16. yes	...
17. take - a walk	...?
18. no	...
19. wash - the cup	...?
20. yes	...

Conversations

Conversation: Music

1. What kind of music do you like?
   a) I like classic music, such as Bach and Mozart.
   b) I love rock music. My favorite band is Godsmack.

2. Do you have an MP3 player?
   a) Yes, I have one, but it is very old.
   b) No, I don't have one, but I can listen to music on my cell phone.

3. How many songs do you have on your computer?
   a) I have around 300 songs on my computer.
   b) I don't know. There are many songs on my computer.

4. When was the last time you listened to music?
   a) I listened to my MP3 player 30 minutes ago.
   b) I listened to music last night just before bed.

5. What song did you listen to recently?
   a) It was Gee by Girls' Generation. I really like that group.
   b) I listened to Queen's song. It's called "We will rock you."

6. Do you like to go to music concerts?
   a) Yes, I do. I like to go to rock music concerts.
   b) No, I don't. I just want to listen to music alone.

7. Who is your favorite singer?

   a) My favorite singer is Queen. I like classic rock.

   b) I like PSY most because he is really funny.

8. Why do you like your favorite singer?

   a) His music has good lyrics.

   b) She has a good voice. It is beautiful.

9. How often do you listen to your favorite singer's songs?

   a) I listen to her songs everyday on my phone.

   b) I listen to his songs when I am depressed.

10. Where do you download music?

    a) I download music from 'Naver Music'.

    b) I usually buy music CDs. CDs have better sound quality.

11. Which do you like better, classic music or jazz music?

    a) I prefer jazz music. It is relaxing.

    b) I like classic music better. It helps reduce my stress.

12. Do you like to listen to music before falling asleep?

    a) Yes, I always listen to music before going to bed.

    b) No, I want to sleep without any sound.

13. Do you like to sing?
    a) Yes, I do. I sometimes go to a karaoke room.
    b) No, I don't. I am not good at singing.

14. What is your favorite musical instrument?
    a) I love the violin because it is so beautiful.
    b) I enjoy the guitar because I love rock music.

15. Which do you prefer, listening to songs or singing songs?
    a) I prefer singing because I have a good voice.
    b) I like both because music makes me feel happy.

16. How often do you download songs from the Internet?

17. Do you ever buy CDs these days?

18. What kind of music do you listen to when you are angry?

19. What radio program do you listen to?

20. Tell me about your favorite song.

Part II

Today's Proverb

"to take me back"

(ex. "Seeing incoming freshman sure takes me back.")

Pronunciation

/z/: Zoo

The /z/ sound is identical to the /s/, however, you will use your voice instead. A good way to practice this sound is to switch between /s/, /z/, and back again. This will help you to realize that /s/ and /z/ have the same tongue placement and require no movement of the tongue or mouth.

Beginning	Middle	End
zoo	Jesus	use
zero	easy	pizzazz
zinc	disease	size
zoom	ozone	series
zebra	desert	cause
zealous	desire	has

1. New items in stores should have pizzazz in their promotions.
2. I thought the test was easy, but my result was a zero.
3. He has a large-size hat that he sometimes wears.
4. Using a computer is not always easy.
5. People often desire to organize their daily lives with planners.
6. The Game of Thrones TV series has many fans.

Drills

Drill #1: Q&A Drill

(plural general and specific pronouns – some/any/them)

Key	Answer
Clean - socks ***Yes***	*Did you clean socks?* *Yes, I cleaned some.*
Buy - the cakes ***no***	*Did you buy the cakes?* *No, I didn't buy them.*

1. sell - hair pins **2. yes**	Did you sell ...? Yes, I ... some.
3. light - the candles **4. no**	Did you light ...? No, ... light them.
5. spend - money **6. yes**	Did you ...? ... some.
7. wear - the earrings **8. no**	Did ... wear the ...? No, ... them.
9. drink - tea **10. no**	... tea? No, ... any.
11. take - the classes **12. yes**	... the classes? ... them.
13. bring - clothes **14. yes**	... clothes? ... some.
15. use - the credit cards **16. yes**	...? ...
17. take - transportation **18. no**	...? ...
19. watch - the movies **20. yes**	...? ...

Drill #2: Transformation

(present progressive → past tense)

Key	Answer
I - do my homework ***Yesterday***	*I am doing my homework.* *I did my homework yesterday.*

Key	Answer
1. She - clean her room **2. last night**	She is cleaning her ... She cleaned her ... last night.
3. They - read a newspaper **4. this morning**	... are reading a newspaper. ... read ... this morning.
5. I - play the violin **6. yesterday**	I am ... I played the violin ...
7. He - take a shower **8. last night**	He is taking ... He took ...
9. She - listen to the radio **10. a little while ago**	... is listening ... .. listened ... a little while ago.
11. We - take a midterm test **12. the day before yesterday**	We are ... We took ...
13. They - wear nice shoes **14. this morning**	They are ... They wore ...
15. You - go to the beach **16. last summer**	... the beach. ... last summer.
17. I - wash the dishes **18. about 10 minutes ago**	... ...
19. She - watch the soccer game **20. last night**	... ...

Drill #3: Article

The Characteristics of High Self-Confidence

(Judy H. Wright (http://www.selfgrowth.com/articles/Characteristics_of_High_Self_Confidence.html))

There are certain characteristics of those who have high self-esteem and confidence in their ability to affect the journey of their life. These factors are universal and can be learned if they are not present in [your] life right now.

1. **They are ambitious.** They want more from life than existence or survival. They can envision themselves in better circumstances and surroundings.
2. **They are goal oriented.** They seek a challenge of completing and setting new goals for themselves. They are not especially competitive, except against themselves. They enjoy breaking their own records.
3. **They are visionary.** Rather than being stuck for too long, they can see themselves in better circumstances and surroundings. They keep a picture of what success will be like.
4. **They have learned to communicate.** They know how to ask for what they want and to hear advice and counsel. It is less important for them to be right than to be effective. They listen more than they speak.
5. **They are loving and kind.** Those people who have a good inner self image form nourishing relationships instead of toxic ones. They have learned to detach from relationships which do not allow them to be authentic.
6. **They are attractive and open to others.** Self-confident people are usually drawn to one another. They vibrate their confidence in a way that attracts good things and good people to them. Being attractive does not necessarily mean physically attractive in the usual sense of the word, but rather spiritually beautiful.

There are also universal characteristics of those who have low self-esteem and lack the confidence to attract abundance in all areas of life to them. These factors often influence the joy that a person may experience.

1. **They are fearful of change.** Many people with low confidence in the future come from a basis of lack and live their life in fear of "what if....." Low confidence people tend to be re–active rather than pro–active.
2. **They are pessimistic and tend to see the glass as half empty.** By blaming circumstances on other people, they delay assuming personal responsibility for their own choices.
3. **They have difficulty communicating what they really want from life.** They have no clear idea of what they value and are muddy about goals and desires. When asked what would make them happy, they give generalities (rich, thin, beautiful) rather than specific ($200,000 a year, wearing size ten boot cut jeans).
4. **They want to please others more than be true to themselves.** The desire to have peace at any price is more important than discovering their own potential. Almost as chameleons, lizards that change colors to fit the environment they are in, those who lack self-confidence would rather blend in than stand out.

> **"Low self-esteem is like driving through life with your handbreak on."**
> - Maxwell Maltz
>
> **"We tend to live to our expectations."**
> - Earl Nightingale

5. **They are insecure and are drawn to others who also see themselves as victims.** They often form destructive and toxic relationships that reflect and increase their lack of self–worth.

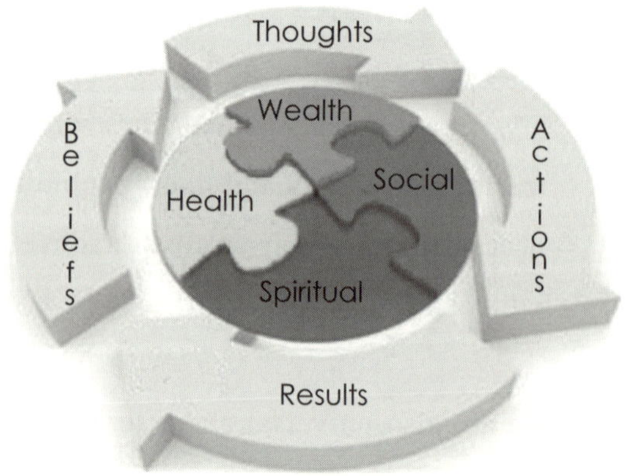

Confidence, self-esteem, or sure knowledge of who you are comes from knowledge of self-inspection. It is an intimate experience and resides in the core of your being. Internal work is the hardest labor you will ever do in your life. There is no greater barrier to strong, healthy, and mutually respectful relationships than lack of confidence.

If you hope to achieve a happy relationship with someone, nothing is more important than healthy self-esteem and confidence, both for you and the other person. Deep-seated feelings that you are not loveable or worthy is a definite roadblock to any relationship.

Discussion Questions:

1. What are your strong points?
2. What are your weak points?
3. Do you have a high self-esteem?
4. What do you think about the 'circle of success'? (see the picture above)
5. Which characteristics from the article do you want to work on?

Conversations

Conversation: Health

1. Do you think you are healthy?
   a) Yes, I do. I exercise everyday at the gym.
   b) No, I don't. I am sick now. I have a cold.

2. Do you want to exercise more?
   a) Yes, I do. I need to exercise more. I am a little overweight.
   b) No, I don't. I don't like to exercise. I hate sweating.

3. Did you have a cold last winter?
   a) Yes, I did. I had runny nose.
   b) No, I didn't. I rarely have a cold.

4. How do you relax?
   a) I usually listen to music. It helps ease my stress.
   b) I do yoga. Stretching feels great.

5. Do you take a vitamin everyday?
   a) Yes, I do. I take one everyday.
   b) No, I don't, but I eat a lot of fruit.

6. How often do you eat fast food?
   a) I eat fast food at least once a week.
   b) I like fast food. I eat fast food every 2 days.

7. Do you eat or drink something special for your health?
   a) Yes, I do. I drink herb tea.
   b) No, I don't. I usually just eat regular food.

8. What Korean food is famous for being a healthy food?
   a) Kimchi is famous for being a healthy food. It has a lot of garlic and ginger.
   b) Red ginseng is the most famous for being a healthy food. It gives you energy.

9. Do you drink mineral water?
   a) Yes, I do. I drink Jeju mineral water.
   b) No, I don't. I drink filtered water.

10. Do you exercise regularly?
    a) Yes, I do. I exercise everyday. I lift weights at home.
    b) No, I don't, but I want to learn yoga.

11. Have you ever joined a health club?
    a) Yes, I have. I used to go to a health club everyday with my brother.
    b) No, I haven't. It looks boring. I prefer dancing.

12. What kind of exercise do you do?
    a) I dance twice a week. I take a dance class.
    b) I swim in a swimming pool every weekend.

13. Have you ever done yoga?
    a) Yes, I have. Yoga is very popular these days.
    b) No, I haven't, but I want to try it.

14. Do you think you are out of shape?
    a) Yes, I do. I think I am a little chubby.
    b) No, I don't. I am in shape. I feel great!

15. Have you ever been to an oriental doctor? Why or why not?

16. What do you do when you have a cold?

17. Have you ever gone on a diet?

18. Where can you buy medicine?

19. What restaurant do you like that cooks healthy food?

20. Tell me how to stay healthy.

Extra Practice:

- Review the previous questions with your group, or ask new questions.
- Try some free talking. Put your notes, papers, and books away and just speak English.

Lesson 10

Pronunciation

Part Ⅰ : /s/

Part Ⅱ : /z/

Drills

Part Ⅰ : Some Basic Marketing Vocabulary Words

Marketing Vocabulary Practice

Part Ⅱ : Adverbs of Frequency

Substitution – past tense

Article – The First Objective of Marketing

Conversations

Part Ⅰ : General Hobbies

Part Ⅱ : Basic Marketing

Part I

Today's Proverb

"Don't brag about yourself – let others praise you." – Proverbs 27:2

Pronunciation

/s/: Sell

(A review of /s/ from Lesson 9.)

Beginning	Middle	End
sell	hassle	mess
simple	outside	purchase
sort	Mr.	harass
sample	Miss	twice
system	Mrs.	yes
success	first	across

1. The secret to success is to maintain your confidence.
2. Many customers enjoy getting free samples prior to purchase.
3. What sort of office supplies do you need?
4. That sounds like a simple plan to reduce costs.
5. I tried to sell something twice but made a mess of things.
6. You should seriously consider studying English.

Drills

Drill #1: Some Basic Marketing Vocabulary Words

a name brand	freebies	after-sales service
a trend	a survey	a retailer
distribution	mass-media	a commercial
advertising/ad	a combo/set	a customer

Drill #2: Marketing Vocabulary Practice

*** Make some sentences using the vocabulary words. ***

ex. "Koreans often try to follow the latest fashion **trends**."

ex. "My favorite **name brand** is Nike."

Conversations

Conversation: General Hobbies

1. Good morning/afternoon/evening. How are you today?
   a) I'm great. I am happy to be in this class today. How are you?
   b) I'm a little tired. I have many classes today.

2. Do you have an English nickname?
   a) Yes, I do. My English nickname is ________.
   b) Yes, I do. My nickname is ____________.

3. What are your hobbies?
   a) My hobbies are playing basketball and ice skating.
   b) I am too busy these days, so my only hobby is sleeping.

4. Why do you like your hobby?
   a) I like sleeping because I study very hard. I'm always very tired.
   b) I enjoy baseball because it is an exciting sport.

5. Where can you play basketball?
   a) You can play basketball in front of the university. There is a basketball court.
   b) I'm not really sure. Sometimes, I play basketball near my apartment in Haeundae.

6. How hard is skiing?
   a) It's not very hard. Many children can ski.
   b) I've been practicing for a long time, but I'm still not good at skiing.

7. How long have you been doing your hobby?
   a) I've been doing my hobby for 11 years. I started when I was in elementary school.
   b) I started doing my hobby 6 months ago when my friend introduced it to me.

8. Who do you usually do your hobbies with?
   a) I usually do my hobbies alone. I enjoy solitude.
   b) I like to do my hobbies with my friends. Isn't that what friends are for?

9. Where is the best place to go ice skating?
   a) I never go ice skating because I'm not good at it, so I don't know where you can go ice skating in this city.
   b) I heard there is a skating rink in Shinsaegae Department Store.

10. Which hobbies are the most popular in your country?
   a) Koreans really love golf and tennis. They are the most popular hobbies.
   b) Many Koreans enjoy hiking because Korea has many mountains and hiking is good for your health.

11. What new hobby do you want to take up?
   a) I want to take up knitting. It's not expensive, and many people enjoy it.
   b) I'm interested in doing a martial art because self-defense is practical.

12. How much does your hobby cost to do?

   a) Knitting is cheap, so it only costs about 10,000 won to start.

   b) Hapkido is expensive because you have to join a dojang. It costs about 90,000 won to take a class for one month.

13. Are you interested in learning how to cook?

   a) Yes, I am. Cooking is very useful. I want to learn to make pizzas.

   b) I already know how to cook. My mother taught me since I was a child.

14. Do you ever play computer games?

   a) Yes, I do. I play computer games everyday. I really love MMO (Massive Multiplayer Online) games and RTS (Real Time Strategy) games.

   b) No, I don't. I don't really have any free time to play games.

15. Do you like to play sports?

   a) No, I just like watching them on TV.

   b) Sure, I always play soccer if I have a chance. I'm very good at soccer.

16. What hobbies are good for families to do together?

17. What new hobbies do you recommend that I take up?

18. Do you think married or dating people need to have the same hobbies?

19. What hobbies are too expensive for you to do?

20. What are some really cheap hobbies?

10

Part Ⅱ

Today's Idiom

"...an arm and a leg."

(ex. "Wow, gas costs an arm and a leg these days.")

Pronunciation

/z/: Zip

(A review of /z/ from Lesson 9.)

Beginning	Middle	End
zip	ozone	as
zap	music	size
zero	pleasant	sneeze
zest	fizzle	days
Zeke	advertising	bosses
zigzag	design	signs

1. Zeke sees the signs advertising the new designs.
2. This car is being sold as—is with zero money down.
3. The firecracker fizzled when the fuse was lit.
4. These days many people are worried about the ozone layer.
5. When my wife bought her wedding dress, it was an American size zero.
6. The pleasant music helped ease my worried mind.

Drills

Drill #1: Adverbs of Frequency

(always, almost always, usually, often, sometimes, not often, rarely, almost never, never)

Key	Answer
play piano	*I usually play the piano* *--- I do too / I don't.*
go swimming	*I always go swimming.* *--- I do too / I don't.*
study	*I almost never study.* *--- I do. / I don't either.*

1. go dancing	**14. do my homework**
2. watch horror movies	**15. go to parties**
3. shop for cosmetics	**16. give money to my parents**
4. buy something online	**17. call my boyfriend/girlfriend**
5. fill out surveys	**18. borrow money**
6. exercise	**19. speak in English**
7. watch TV commercials	**20. try to make new friends**
8. eat lunch at school	**21. play badminton**
9. meet people from the Internet	**22. buy name brands**
10. go drinking with my friends	**23. fight with my parents**
11. get into trouble	**24. wear casual clothes**
12. smoke	**25. go out to eat**
13. study for a test	**26. eat fast food**

Drill #2: Substitution Drill

(past tense)

Key	Answer
I go to school - yesterday	*I went to school yesterday.*
last week	*I went to school last week.*
the park	*I went to the park last week.*
1. We	We went to the park last week.
2. They	They went to the park last week.
3. an hour ago	They … to the park an hour ago.
4. run	They ran ...
5. swim	They swam ...
6. last month	… last month.
7. go to Seoul	…went to Seoul last month.
8. last winter	They went to Seoul ...
9. He	… Seoul last winter.
10. study	He studied ...
11. dance	He ...
12. I	I ...
13. sing	I sang ...
14. just before class	I …just before class.
15. see - the professor	I saw the professor ...
16. talk - to my friend	...
17. on Wednesday	...
18. watch TV	...
19. see a good movie	...
20. take a test	...
21. read a book	...
22. last weekend	…
23. We	…
24. drop by your house	...

Drill #3: Article

The First Objective of Marketing

(Kerin, Hartley, Berkowitz, and Rudelius. Marketing 8th ed., NY: McGraw–Hill/Irwin, 2006.)

Maslow's Hierarchy of Needs

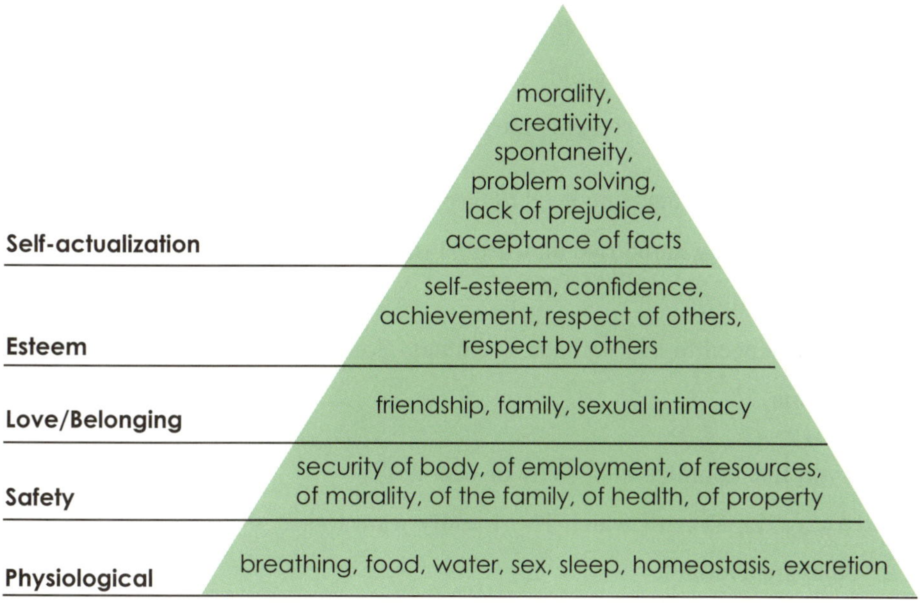

From : Wikipedia – Spring 2007

"The first objective in marketing is discovering the needs of consumers. This is not easy because consumers may not always know or be able to tell you what they want. A person feels a need when they don't have a basic necessity such as food, clothing, and shelter. A want is something we feel we need because of our culture, knowledge, or personality. Effective marketing tries to influence what consumers want and what they buy."

Conversations

Conversation: Basic Marketing

1. What are some things you want to buy?
   a) I want to buy a new cell phone because mine is really old. I want to buy some new shoes too. I really like Nike, so I want to buy that brand.
   b) My computer is really old, so I want to upgrade it. I want to buy a really fast computer that can play movies, games, and music well.

2. What are some things you need to buy?
   a) I need to buy some rice and fruit. I only have a little rice and no fruit in my apartment.
   b) I really need to buy some new clothes. Some of my clothes are too small for me.

3. Do you like commercials? Why or why not?
   a) Yes, I do. When I watch TV, I really want to see all of the new products that are available.
   b) No, I don't. I really wish TV didn't have so many commercials. I always get angry when I see them.

4. Do you like advertisements on the subway or bus?
   a) Yes, I do. They give me something to look at so that I'm not bored.
   b) No, I don't. There are too many, and I especially hate the music they play over the speaker system.

5. Where do you like to shop?
   a) I like to shop at department stores, like Lotte Department Store. There are many places to shop and products to buy.
   b) I usually shop online. I think Internet shopping malls are the best places to shop.

6. Where did you buy your shirt?
   a) I bought it at Hyundai Department Store. It was fashionable, and I liked it.
   b) I didn't buy this shirt. My mom bought it for me.

7. Do you ever research a product online before you buy it?
   a) Yes, I do. I usually like to check online to find out some information first.
   b) No, I don't. I often go to the store and just ask questions.

8. Where did you buy those shoes?
   a) I bought these shoes at Lotte Department Store. They were a good price.
   b) I ordered them from an online shopping mall.

9. Do you like to shop online?
   a) Yes, I do. Shopping online is my favorite hobby. I often buy things online.
   b) Sometimes, I do. I shop online when I have free time. I usually just visit stores near my house.

10. What products do you like to shop for?
    a) I really like shopping for new cell phones. I always want to find out about the new features and styles.
    b) I often go shopping for cosmetics. It takes me a long time to pick the best ones for me.

11. Have you ever sold anything? (Also ask #12.)
    a) Yes, I have. I sold my old bicycle to a neighbor for 50,000 won.
    b) No, I haven't. I tried to sell my used textbooks, but nobody wanted to buy them.

12. How did you market what you sold?
    a) I just went to my neighbor and asked if he needed a bicycle. I asked him if he wanted to buy mine for 50,000 won, and he agreed.
    b) I posted on a message board, but nobody emailed me.

13. Do you think you are a good salesperson?
    a) Yes, I do. I can sell anything. Would you like to buy this pen?
    b) No, I don't. I'm too shy, and I often forget important things to say.

14. What kind of marketing is most effective on you?
    a) I think word-of-mouth is the most effective advertising on me. When I hear about a good product from my friend, I really want to buy it.
    b) Commercials on TV really affect me. I always want to buy something I see on TV.

15. What do you think about flyers people hand out on the street?
    a) I really hate those flyers. They are just trash.
    b) I like those flyers. They give me good information about new stores.

16. What's your favorite commercial on TV these days?

17. How much money do you usually spend when you go shopping?

18. Where can I find information about a new car?

19. Do you watch movie previews at the theater or do you usually ignore them?

20. What makes Korean marketing unique?

Extra Practice:

– Review the previous questions with your group, or ask new questions
– How are marketing styles different in other countries?
– Why do Koreans pronounce "Hyundai" and "Samsung" differently than other countries' peoples?
– Try to do this self–test without looking at the answers:

(**The First Objective of (M)______________________**)

The first objective in (m)____________ is discovering the (n)____________ of consumers. This is not easy because consumers may not always know or be able to tell you what they (w)____________. A person feels a need when they don't have a basic (n)__________ such as (f)____________, (c)____________, and (s)____________. A (w)____________ is something we feel we need because of our (c)____________, (kn)____________, or (p)____________. Effective marketing tries to (i)__________ what consumers want and what they (b)__________.

Lesson 11

Pronunciation

Part I : /Š/ or /sh/

Part II : /Č/ or /ch/

Drills

Part I : Q&A – "What kind(s)... " & "one(s)" + adjective practice

Substitution - past, present, future tense of "be"

Part II : Q&A – making a basic short answer

Q&A – contrary adjectives

Conversations

Part I : Consumer Behavior (Decision Making)

Part II : Daily Life

Part I

Today's Proverb

"All that glitters is not gold."

Vocabulary Words

Trade, Distribution, Business Administration, Management

Pronunciation

/Š/ or /sh/: Share

To make the /Š/ sound effectively, you fold up the sides of your tongue. The middle of your tongue should be near the middle roof of your mouth and the tip of your tongue will be down. This is similar to the /s/ sound, but move your tongue deeper into your mouth. Do not move your lips during the formation of the sound.

Beginning	Middle	End
share	function	English
should	intuition	fish
shall	deception	wash
shard	correction	crush
shrimp	special	cash
shoot	administration	rush

1. I purchased three shares in a fishing company.
2. English shouldn't be too harsh if you study hard.
3. Wash your hands after you rush to the restroom.
4. Women have a special insight that we call "a woman's intuition".
5. The two ships crashed into the shore.
6. She shared her shrimp with her friend.

11

Drills

Drill #1: Q&A

(what kind/kinds – one/ones) + adjective practice

Key	Answer
books	*What kinds of books do you want?* *--- I want thick ones.*
pencil	*What kind of pencil do you want?* *---I want a sharp one.*
1. car	What kind of car do ... want? --- I want a ... one.
2. computer	What kind of ... wnat? --- I want ... one.
3. pens	... kinds of pens ... --- I want ... ones.
4. bag	... kind of ... want? --- I want a ...
5. friends	What kinds ... --- ones.
6. professor	... kind professor ... --- I want a ...
7. camera	... kind ... --- I ...
8. shirt	... ...
9. pants	... ...
10. pillows	... ...
11. house	... ...
12. job	... ...

13. homework assignments	… …
14. bicycle	… …
15. hats	… …

Drill #2: Substitution Drill

(to be - past, present, and future tenses)

Key	Answer
She is tired - yesterday	*She was tired yesterday.*
tomorrow – (question)	*Will she be tired tomorrow?*
you	*Will you be tired tomorrow?*
now	*Are you tired now?*
he	*Is he tired now?*
1. sleepy	Is he sleepy now?
2. (negative)	Isn't he … now?
3. angry	Isn't he …?
4. studying	Isn't … studying now?
5. next week	Won't … be studying next week?
6. (affirmative)	Will he be …?
7. (statement)	He will ….
8. you	You … next week.
9. taking a test	… be taking … week.
10. yesterday	…were taking ...
11. today	… taking … today.
12. I	I am ...
13. sleepy	I ...
14. (negative)	I … not ...
15. he	He's not ...
16. (question)	Isn't … today?
17. tonight	Won't he be …?
18. she	…?

19. angry	…?
20. (affirmative)	…?
21. going home	…?
22. dancing	…?
23. I	…?
24. (statement)	…

Conversations

Conversation: Consumer Behavior (Decision Making)

1. Why don't people always buy things online?
    a) Because they can't see the products very easily.
    b) It is difficult to trust online stores. Sometimes, the products are not good.

2. Which is better, Coke, Pepsi, or Chilsung Cider?
    a) I think Coke is best. I always buy Coke when I go out.
    b) I like Chilsung Cider because it tastes better than cola.

3. How do you feel about Nike?
    a) I feel that Nike is famous for sports clothing. Many athletes wear Nike.
    b) I just think that Nike is too expensive for normal people. I don't buy it.

4. Do you ever use a credit card?
    a) Yes, I do. I often use a credit card when I go shopping.
    b) No, I don't. I usually just use cash when I buy something.

5. What is something you want to buy soon?
   a) I really want to buy a new car. I am saving my money for one.
   b) I want to buy a new computer. My computer is too slow.

6. Where do you prefer to shop?
   a) I prefer to shop in a department store. They have a wider selection of products.
   b) I like shopping online. I can find anything I need on the Internet at a good price.

7. Why do you prefer to shop at your favorite store?
   a) I like seeing all of the different products. I can try on clothes, ask questions, and walk around to get exercise, so I like department stores.
   b) The Internet is really easy to use. I can research product information, find the cheapest price, and relax while I'm shopping.

8. Do you use coupons or mileage cards?
   a) Yes, I do. I always use my OK Cashback card.
   b) I sometimes use a coupon when I buy something from the supermarket.

9. Do you prefer to buy domestic brands or foreign brands?
   a) I like buying domestic brands, like Samsung. It's easier to get service for them.
   b) I like foreign brands more. They have a better brand image and are usually good quality.

10. What product do you research before buying?
    a) I usually research electronics before buying them. I don't want to buy a defective product.
    b) These days I am reading up on different cars. I want to buy a good car soon.

11. Where do you do research for a product you want to buy?
   a) I always search for product information online. It's fast, easy, and fun.
   b) I usually talk to the salesperson at the store. They know many things about the products that I want to buy.

12. Do you have any brand loyalties?
   a) I don't care about any specific brands. I just buy whatever is good.
   b) I really love Coke. I hate Pepsi and Chilsung Cider. Coke is number one.

13. How do you learn about new products?
   a) I learn about new products when I watch television. Commercials are always on during my favorite TV shows.
   b) My friends usually tell me about new products.

14. Why did you return a product?
   a) I returned a shirt because it was too small for me.
   b) I had to take back my tablet. It didn't work when I bought it.

15. Have you ever repaired your cell phone?

16. How do you feel after buying an expensive product?

17. What factors will you consider when you buy an apartment?

18. If you had 1,000,000 won, what would you buy?

image from koreatimes.co.kr

19. What factors are most important to you when you buy a car?

20. Do you prefer name brands or saving money by buying unknown brands?

Part Ⅱ

Today's Idiom

"... to text some one."

(ex. I'll text you late.)

Pronunciation

/Č/ or /ch/: Cheap

To make the /ch/ sound, you need to do the same thing as /sh/ but push the tip of your tongue all the way up to stop your air flow. Then, drop your tongue down quickly into the /sh/ position to make this sound.

Beginning	Middle	End
cheap	purchase	snatch
charming	question	itch
choose	teacher	leech
chase	situation	such
check	furniture	niche
charge	pitcher	speech

1. Do you want to pay with cash, check, or charge?
2. The furniture that you purchased is very cheap.
3. I have an itch that I can't scratch.
4. This is a situation where such a change is required.
5. Every company searches for a niche in the market.
6. My teacher asked a question about my speech.

Drills

Drill #1: Question and Quick Answers

(making a basic short answer)

Key	Answer
Is the apple red?	*Yes, it is.*
Are you unhappy?	*No, I'm not.*
Are the pens blue?	*Yes, they are.*

1. Is there a car in the garage?	Yes, there …
2. Is it raining?	No, … isn't.
3. Are you going to school?	…, I am.
4. Do you like kimchi?	Yes, …
5. Don't you like kimchi?	…, I do.
6. Were you at school yesterday?	… wasn't.
7. Am I a student?	Yes, …
8. Is his name "John"?	No, …
9. Is your book thick?	Yes, …
10. Are you parents tired?	…
11. Isn't there a pencil on the desk?	…
12. Are they good students?	…
13. Is she a nice girl?	…
14. Will you help me?	…
15. Do you like his hat?	…
16. Are you cold?	…
17. Is Korea a great country?	…
18. Are there any students in this class?	…
19. Is there a bathroom on this floor?	…
20. Do you have a headache?	…
21. Can I borrow your pencil?	…
22. Is our university large?	…

Drill #2: Question and Answer Drill

(contrary adjectives)

Key	Answer
"Kang, Ho-dong" - weak	*Is Kang, Ho-dong weak?* *No, he isn't. He's strong.*
the movie - interesting	*Is the movie interesting?* *No, it isn't. It's boring.*
1. this class - long	Is this class long? No, it isn't. It's short.
2. that cat - old	Is that cat old? No, it isn't. It's young.
3. this cherry - bitter	Is … bitter? No, … It's sweet.
4. his water bottle - full	Is his … full? No, … It's empty.
5. that train - fast	… fast? … It's slow
6. this shirt - dirty	… dirty? … clean.
7. John - married	…? … single.
8. this library - public	… …
9. the test - easy	… …
10. the bag - heavy	… …
11. this dog - noisy	… …
12. the actor - popular	… …

13. this cat - sick	… …
14. the country - dangerous	… …
15. this food - spicy	… …

Conversations

Conversation: Daily Life

1. What time do you wake up in the morning?
   a) I wake up early every day to get ready for school.
   b) I wake up around 10am to get ready for school.

2. Do you always eat breakfast?
   a) No, I don't. I never eat breakfast these days.
   b) Yes, I do. My mother always cooks breakfast for the family.

3. What is your favorite food for breakfast?
   a) My favorite food for breakfast is donuts. I sometimes buy Dunkin' Donuts when I come to class.
   b) I really like soup and fish for breakfast. I think it is very healthy and gives me energy.

4. What time did you come to school?
   a) I arrived at school at 9am for my accounting class.
   b) I got here around 12pm to talk to my friends before class.

5. Where do you usually eat lunch?
   a) I usually go home to eat. My mom cooks lunch for me.
   b) I don't have much free time, so I eat at the school cafeteria on weekdays.

6. How long does your homework usually take to finish?
   a) My homework usually takes about 1 or 2 hours to finish every night.
   b) I have about 10 hours of homework every week.

7. What is your hardest class?
   a) My hardest class is this class. English is really hard for me.
   b) Consumer Behavior with Professor Choi is my hardest class. He's really strict.

8. What time will you go home?
   a) I'll probably head home around 6pm this evening.
   b) I'm going out with my friends tonight, so I won't go home until after midnight.

9. What things do you enjoy doing at home?
   a) I like playing computer games, studying, and watching TV at home.
   b) My favorite things to do at home are sleep, eat, and talk to my family.

10. Do you usually eat supper at home or go out to eat?
   a) I have to eat supper at home because my mom cooks food for me everyday.
   b) I usually go out to eat with my friends. We often eat "kimbob" together for supper.

11. When do you take a shower?
   a) I take a shower every morning before class.
   b) I like to take showers at night, so I can go to bed clean.

12. How much water do you drink every day?
   a) I try to drink at least 4 or 5 glasses of water every day.
   b) I almost never drink any water. I usually just drink tea or pop.

13. Do you exercise these days?
    a) Yes, I do. I always play soccer with my friends between classes.
    b) No, I don't. I should probably join a gym, but I don't have enough time.

14. How long does it take you to get home from here?
    a) If I walk home from here, it takes me about 30 minutes.
    b) If I take the bus from here, it takes me one hour to get home.

15. How long does it take you to get ready in the morning?

16. How long does it take you to fall asleep at night?

17. Do you ever go to bed late?

18. Do your parents get angry if you stay out late?

19. What kind of house chores do you do at home?

20. Have you ever cooked for your whole family? What did you cook?

Extra Practice:

- Review the previous questions with your group, or ask new questions
- What is "consumer behavior"?
- Why should we study "consumer behavior"?
- Why do companies give away freebies with a purchase?
- Why is it important for companies to advertise often?
- What do you think about Pepsi? Reebok? Gucci? BMW? Marlboro? Samsung? Iriver?
- What are some strategies companies use to attract consumers?
- Can you name any stores or businesses in your neighborhood that have failed? Why do you think they failed?
- Can you think of any way to advertise effectively on the Internet?

Lesson 12

Pronunciation

Part Ⅰ : /ks/

Part Ⅱ : /gz/

Drills

Part Ⅰ : Substitution – "to be" – verb tense
Substitution – personal qualities

Part Ⅱ : Sentence Transformation – "How much..." & "cost"
Q&A – "What did you buy?" & monetary amounts

Conversations

Part Ⅰ : Consumer Behavior (Understanding the Buyers)

Part Ⅱ : Technology

Part I

Today's Proverb

"...whatever one sows, that will he also reap..." --- Galations 6:7
(or more commonly: "You reap what you sow.")

Pronunciation

/ks/: Asks

Quickly combine /k/ and /s/ in order to pronounce an 'x' or 'ks' in English.

Beginning	Middle	End
-	axis	asks
-	excite	knick-knacks
-	experience	fax
-	taxes	Turks
-	mixer	complex
-	boxing	hacks

1. The kick boxer asks about the excitement of the match.
2. Taxes are complex for him because he never asks for help.
3. I live in an apartment complex on East Colfax.
4. The experience of shopping for knick–knacks was taxing.
5. The cracks in the rocks were along the same axis.
6. The schedule for the mixer came by fax.

Drills

Drill #1: Substitution Drill

(to be – verb tense)

Key	Answer
cheap	*It's cheap today.*
yesterday	*It was cheap yesterday.*

1. tomorrow	It will be cheap tomorrow.
2. cheaper	It will be cheaper tomorrow.
3. next week	It … cheaper next week.
4. on sale	It will be on sale ...
5. discounted	… discounted next week.
6. promoted	It will be promoted ...
7. the day before yesterday	It was … the day before yesterday.
8. last month	It was ....
9. sold out	…was sold out ...
10. in stock	… in stock last month.
11. right now	It is …now.
12. out of stock	It … out of stock ...
13. full price	… full price ...
14. last weekend	It was ...
15. next Monday	… will be ...
16. half-price	.. will … next ...
17. 50% off	It …be 50% off ...
18. more expensive	It … next Monday.
19. 30% off	It … next Monday.
20. a steal	It ... a steal … Monday.
21. in December	It … December.
22. 15% off	It is ...
23. in July	It is … July.
24. on display	… in July.
25. advertised	…
26. offered	…
27. sold	…
28. given away	…
29. next December	…
30. on the weekend	…

Drill #2: Substitution Drill

(personal qualities)

Key	Answer
She - kind - boss	*She is a kind boss.*
warm	*She is a warm boss.*
He	*He is a warm boss.*
1. generous	He is a … boss.
2. optimistic	He is an optimistic ...
3. supervisor	He is … optimistic supervisor.
4. easy-going	He … easy-going supervisor.
5. employee	He is … easy-going ...
6. hard-working	… a hard-working employee.
7. diligent	… diligent employee.
8. employer	… employer.
9. suspicious	He is ...
10. thrifty	He … employer.
11. customer	He is a ....
12. honest	… an honest ...
13. clever	… a … customer.
14. She	She ..clever ...
15. concerned	…
16. angry	…
17. satisfied	…
18. They	…
19. consumer	…
20. I	....
21. manager	…
22. extroverted	…
23. lazy	…
24. introverted	…
25. thoughtful	…
26. She	…
27. reliable	…
28. flexible	…
29. good	…
30. careful	…

Conversations

Conversation: Consumer Behavior (Understanding the Buyers)

1. Why do customers sometimes get angry?
   a) Customers sometimes get angry because the salesperson is rude.
   b) I think customers get angry because the product isn't what they expected.

2. Why do customers search online for product information?
   a) I think customers search online because there is a lot of information on the Internet.
   b) I almost never use the Internet, so I don't know why customers search online.

3. Why do customers return products after buying?
   a) Customers return products after buying because the products are sometimes defective.
   b) Sometimes, customers are not satisfied with their products after buying them, so they return the product.

4. Where else do customers learn about new products?
   a) A customer can learn about new products by going shopping.
   b) Customers can learn about new products by reading some magazines they are interested in.

5. Why does it take a long time to shop for clothes but not for snacks?
   a) Clothes are important and snacks are not, so people shop carefully for clothes.
   b) I think clothes are more expensive than snacks, so people take a long time to shop for clothes.

6. Is buying a cell phone a big purchase decision?
   a) Yes, it is. Cell phones are expensive, and it takes a long time to choose one.
   b) No it isn't. These days, cell phones are not expensive, and they are all similar.

7. Do you sometimes put off (delay) buying something you really want?
   a) I often delay buying something I want so I can find a good deal.
   b) No, I don't. I usually buy something I want as soon as I can.

8. What kind of a shopper are you?
   a) I am a careful shopper. I often look for the best quality and price.
   b) I'm a big spender. I usually spend a lot of money when I go shopping.

9. Why do some people hate buying products online?
   a) Online stores are not always good. Sometimes, the products are different than the picture on the website.
   b) It's difficult to shop online because you must know about computers and Internet banking well.

10. Have you ever gone shopping in another country? If so, tell about your experience.
   a) No, I haven't, but I'd like to go shopping in New York.
   b) Yes, I have. I went shopping in London. The prices of everything were so expensive, but there were many good products to buy.

11. Why do men usually shop faster than women?
   a) Men are more interested in sports and relaxing. They don't like to spend money.
   b) Women care a lot about image. They want to find a product that matches their personality well.

12. Who makes the big purchase decisions in your family?
    a) My father always makes the final decision to buy something expensive in my family.
    b) Our family decides what to buy together when the product is very expensive.

13. Do you ever buy on impulse?
    a) No, I don't. I always consider my purchase carefully before I spend my money.
    b) Yes, I do. I sometimes buy something I see in the store without thinking about it very much.

14. Why do customers love discounts and coupons?
    a) Customers are always trying to save money, so they love discounts and coupons.
    b) Not all customers love discounts and coupons. They are sometimes a hassle.

15. If you were a manager, how could you learn more about your customers?
    a) I could call my customers to ask them about their shopping experience.
    b) I could give my customers a survey with many questions.

16. Do you think online shoppers are more satisfied than regular shoppers? Why or why not?

17. If you could open a store, what kind of store do you want to open?

18. Do you think customers are too picky these days?

19. Do you agree with this famous expression: "The customer is always right"?

image is Stew Leonard's Supermarket Customer Service Stone

20. Where is your favorite place to shop?

Part Ⅱ

Today's Idiom

"Murphy's Law - Anything that can go wrong, will go wrong."

Pronunciation

/gz/: Examples

Quickly combine /g/ and /z/ in order to pronounce an 'x' or 'gs' in English.

Beginning	Middle	End
-	examples	plugs
-	exactly	hugs
-	exit	bags
-	exhausted	blogs
-	exempt	cyborgs
-	exalt	hotdogs

1. Hogs are just large pigs.
2. You aren't exempt from carrying bags when you are exiting the store.
3. I exhausted my supply of hotdogs while reading the web blogs.
4. The dogs tore apart the bags at exactly 1 o'clock sharp.
5. Frogs eat bugs and lay eggs in bogs.
6. In Terminator, humans exact revenge on cyborgs.

12

Drills

Drill #1: Sentence Transformation

(Past tense - "How much was/were..." with "cost")

Key	Answer
your shoes ***--- 60,000 won***	*How much were your shoes?* *--- They cost 60,000 won.*
your pen ***--- 3,000 won***	*How much was your pen?* *--- It cost 3,000 won.*

1. that book **2. --- 35,000 won**	How much was that book? --- It cost 35,000 won.
3. those pants **4. --- 65,000 won**	How much were those pants? --- They cost 65,000 won.
5. this cell phone **6. --- 100,000 won**	How much was this cell phone? --- It cost 100,000 won.
7. your pencil **8. --- 500 won**	How … was your pencil? --- It cost 500 ...
9. your electronic dictionary **10. --- 70,000 won**	How … your electronic dictionary? --- … 70,000 won.
11. your mp3 player **12. --- 50,000 won**	How much was …? --- It cost ...
13. her jacket **14. --- about 150,000 won**	… was her jacket? --- … about 150,000 won.
15. his hat **16. --- 20,000 won**	How … his hat? --- It … won.
17. that old car **18. --- 5,000,000 won**	… that old car? --- It ...
19. your new computer **20. --- 1,000,000 won**	How …? --- It ...
21. this bicycle **22. --- 300,000 won**	…? --- ...
23. that lipstick **24. --- 13,000 won**	…? --- ...

25. that bag **26. --- 10,000 won**	…was …? --- … cost ...
27. your glasses **28. --- 120,000 won**	… were …? --- They …
29. your notebooks **30. --- 1,800 won**	…? --- ...

Drill #2: Question and Answer Drill

(What did you buy?)

Key	Answer
--- ***glasses - 120,000 won***	*What did you buy?* *I bought glasses for 120,000 won.*
--- ***books - 50,000 won***	*What did you buy?* *I bought books for 50,000 won.*

1. --- **pencils - 5,000 won**	What did you …? I bought pencils for 5,000 won.
2. --- **a computer - 1,500,000 won**	What did you buy? I bought a computer … 1,500,000 won.
3. --- **a jump rope - 10,000 won**	What … buy? I bought … for 10,000 won.
4. --- **a cup - 1,000 won**	What … buy? I … 1,000 won.
5. --- **a printer - 45,000 won**	What …? I bought … won.
6. --- **a new watch - 80,000 won**	…buy? I … for 80,000 won.
7. --- **computer paper - 5,000 won**	…? I … 5,000 won.
8. --- **a new TV - 900,000 won**	…? …

9. --- **some kimchi - 3,000 won**	... ? ...
10. --- **eye shadow - 9,000 won**	...? ....
11. --- **a bottle of Pepsi - 1,000 won**	...? ... a bottle of Pepsi ...
12. --- **a cheese pizza - 5,000 won**	...? ....
13. --- **a pencil case - 1,500 won**	...? ... a pencil ...
14. --- **Nike shoes - 150,000 won**	...? ....
15. --- **a Basic House shirt - 20,000 won**	...? ....

Conversations

Conversation: Technology

1. Do you have a smartphone?
   a) Yes, I do. I have a Samsung smartphone. It's a galaxy S5.
   b) No, I don't. I have an old cell phone. It's a Note 2.

2. How much is your cell phone bill?
   a) It costs about 55,000 won per month.
   b) I pay under 30,000 won a month.

3. Where is a good place to buy a smartphone?
   a) I think a good place to buy a smartphone is near the university.
   b) The best place to buy a smartphone is on the Internet.

4. How do you feel about new technology?
   a) I always like to read news about new technology.
   b) I don't want to learn about new things. New technology is very confusing.

5. Why is new technology very expensive?
   a) The latest products use very expensive parts, so the price is often high.
   b) I think new technology is overpriced because stores are trying to make a profit.
6. When do you want to get a new computer?
   a) I want to get a new computer very soon. My old computer is too slow.
   b) I will wait until my current computer is broken before I buy a new one.
7. Where is a good place to learn about new technology?
   a) I like to search the Internet to learn about new technology.
   b) My friends and family usually tell me about new technology.
8. What new tech gadgets are you excited about?
   a) I'm excited about the new Apple smartphone that is coming out soon.
   b) These days, I don't know much about any new tech gadgets that are coming out.
9. Which company is famous for creating new technological products?
   a) Samsung is famous for new technological products, such as cell phones and computers.
   b) Microsoft always releases new versions of Windows, so I think they are famous for creating new tech.
10. Do you want to have a car that drives itself?
    a) No, I don't. I prefer to drive the car rather than let the computer drive.
    b) Yes, I do. I think that letting the computer drive the car is safer than having a human driver.
11. Are you ever worried that technology can cause problems?
    a) Yes, I am. Sometimes, technology is very scary. Have you seen the movie "Terminator"?
    b) No, I'm not. If technology causes a problem, consumers will demand a solution quickly.

12. Why is flying safer than driving?
    a) These days, airplanes are safer because computers are very advanced. Pilots depend on these computers to fly the airplanes.
    b) I think that pilots are trained very diligently, but drivers are very careless.

13. How often do you use the Internet?
    a) I always use the Internet. My smartphone has Internet access.
    b) I use the Internet for about one hour every day to do my homework.

14. Is it ok for students to study with smartphones?
    a) No, it isn't. Students who use smartphones in class can cheat on exams.
    b) Yes, it is. Smartphones are a useful tool for studying and can help improve our grades.

15. What technology do you love most?

16. What will technology be like in 10 years?

17. What is the most popular mobile device these days?

18. Why are some people afraid of new technology?

19. Do you think it's good that many people have a camera in society?

20. Why do people usually read news on the Internet instead of buying a newspaper?

Extra Practice:

- Review the previous questions with your group, or ask new questions.
- Discuss two different brands, like Samsung and Apple. Why are they different? Which one do you prefer?
- Have you seen any advertisements in foreign countries? Were they different or similar to Korean advertisements?
- What are famous Korean companies that people in foreign countries know?
- In America, Samsung is sometimes considered to be a cheap, low quality

product. Why do you think this is true?
- What brand of car do you want to buy? Why do you want that brand?
- What do you think about Hyundai cars?
- Do you think re-unification with North Korea will help or hurt Korea's global image?

Fun Questions for Extra Practice:
- If zombies attacked your city, how would you survive? Where would you go? What would you take with you? Who would you take with you?
- If your spouse were a vampire, would you let him/her make you a vampire too or would you kill him/her?
- If you could be on a TV program, what program would you be on? Why?
- If someone offered you 100,000 won to wear clown clothes and makeup at school for one day, would you accept?
- If you were superman, would you hide your true identity and pretend to be Clark Kent or would you tell everybody?
- If you were a billionaire, what would you do? Would you be batman?
- If you were a dog, what kind of dog would you be?
- If you had one special power, such as flying, super strength, being a super genius, etc., what power do you want to have?
- What is something you want to do before you die?
- What age would you like to be forever? Why?

Lesson 13

Pronunciation

Part Ⅰ : /u/

Part Ⅱ : /U/

Drills

Part Ⅰ : Q&A – borrowing items

Article – Differences between Domestic Marketing and International Marketing

Part Ⅱ : Substitution – possessive pronouns

Q&A – contrary adjectives

Conversations

Part Ⅰ : Distribution Channels

Part Ⅱ : Communication

13

Part I

Today's Proverb

"What goes around, comes around."

Pronunciation

/u/: Mood

To make the /u/ sound, you make a small circle with your mouth, relax your tongue, and use your voice.

Beginning	Middle	End
-	mood	blue
-	intrude	new
-	who's	grew
-	lewd	too
-	tools	slew
-	troop	true

1. Who's in the mood to eat some new food?
2. I only see you once in a blue moon.
3. It's true that he grew two prunes.
4. The fool ruled the country with his troops.
5. Who threw the noodles in the pool?
6. This cool fruit grew near the lagoon.

Drills

Drill #1: Q&A Practice

(borrowing items)

Key	Answer
1. a pencil ***(Negative Answer)*** ***--- or--- (Affirmative Answer)***	*Do you have a pencil that I could borrow?* *No, I'm afraid I don't have one.* *--- or--- Yes, I have one right here.*
2. money ***(Negative Answer)*** ***--- or --- (Affirmative Answer)***	*Do you have any money that I could borrow?* *No, I'm afraid I don't have any.* *---or--- Yes, I have some right here.*

1. paper	**7. clothes**
2. spare change	**8. sugar**
3. a notebook	**9. a watch**
4. pens	**10. a flash drive**
5. a bag	**11. a tape measure**
6. a stapler	**12. an umbrella**

Drill #2: Article

Differences between Domestic Marketing and International Marketing

When marketing across international borders, it is important for marketers to consider various factors such as cultural differences and language barriers. Simple mistakes in advertisements, sign boards, brand slogans, or even brand names can cause problems for a company when entering an international market. Advertisements and promotional materials need to take into consideration the differences in languages, gestures, cultural identities, religions, habits, and other expressions. Marketers should always get a native speaker or trusted expert who is fluent in the language and culture to check any advertising messages before going public with the material. The following are a list highlighting of some of the differences between English used in the U.S. and English used in Australia and England.

United States	Australia & England
air conditioner / A/C	air conditioner / air con
bar	pub
(car) hood	(car) bonnet
(car) trunk	(car) boot
(car) windshield	(car) windscreen
college / university	university / uni
cracker	biscuit
elementary school	primary school
flashlight	torch / flashlight
fries / French fries	chips
gas	petrol / fuel
garbage can / trash can	rubbish bin / bin
motorcycle	motorbike
pharmacy / drugstore	chemist / chemist's shop
porch / deck	veranda
restroom / public bathroom	public toilet / loo
scarf	muffler [England] / scarf [Australian]
sidewalk	footpath
soccer	football [England] / soccer [Australian]
studio apartment	flat
sweater	jumper

Even when advertising within Korea, companies should be aware that making simple mistakes on their signs or advertisements can make the company seem unconcerned, sloppy, or uneducated. Taking the extra time to make sure that any use of a foreign language is correct, even in a domestic setting, could help to protect or even improve a brand image. Below, there are a few words, phrases, and expressions that are misused in Korea while speaking English and are often referred to as "Konglish". Some expressions may have several English translations depending on the circumstance of their use.

Konglish	Correct English
"A/S" / "after service"	after-sales service / service / repair
"agashi"	Miss / ma'am / a young woman
"ajumma"	Ms. / ma'am / a middle-aged woman
"ajusshi"	Mister / sir / a middle-aged man
"apart"	an apartment / an apartment building
"arubite" [arbeit (German)]	a part-time job / a temporary job
"back mirror"	a rear-view mirror
"bond"	super glue
"cider"	lemon-lime soda
"consent"	an (electrical) outlet / a (electrical) socket
"cunning"	cheating
"depart"	a department store
"driver"	a screwdriver
"Dutch pay"	go Dutch
"eye shopping"	window shopping
"family name"	a surname / a last name
"Fighting!"	"Fight!" / "Do your best!"
"gips"	a cast / a plaster cast
"hagwon" / "institute" / "academy" / etc.	a learning center / a cram school
"halaboji" / "halmoni"	an elderly man / an elderly woman
"hand phone"	a cell phone
"M.T." / "membership training"	a retreat
"officetel" / "one room"	a studio apartment / a flat
"otobai" / "autobi"	a motorcycle / a moped / a motorbike
"oh bite" / "overeat"	vomit / throw up / puke
"one piece"	a dress
"PC bang" / "PC room"	an Internet café
"panty"	underwear / (man) boxers or briefs / (woman) panties

"self"	self service
"sharp"	a mechanical pencil
"short pants"	shorts
"toast"	an egg sandwich / an omelet sandwich
"white"	white out / correction tape
"wrap"	plastic wrap

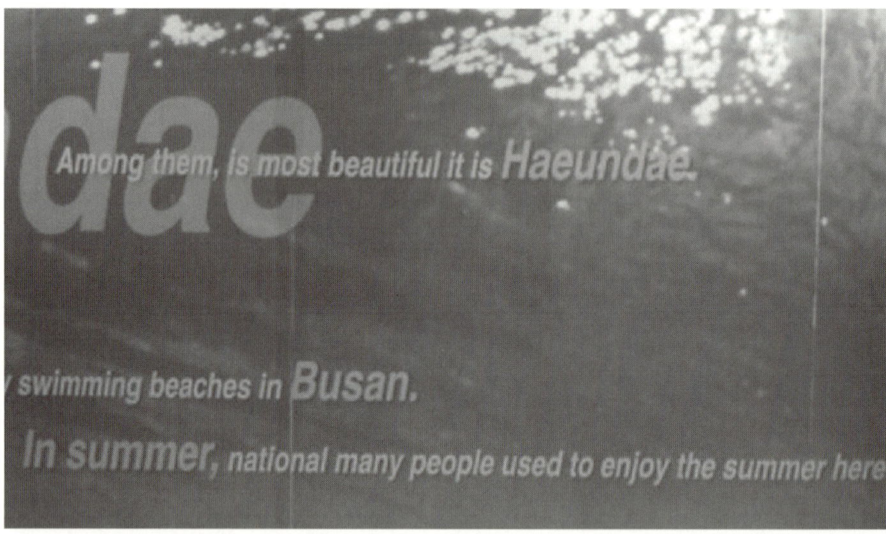

[corrected version] "Among them (the beaches of Busan), the most beautiful is Haeundae." and "Many Korean people enjoy the summers here."

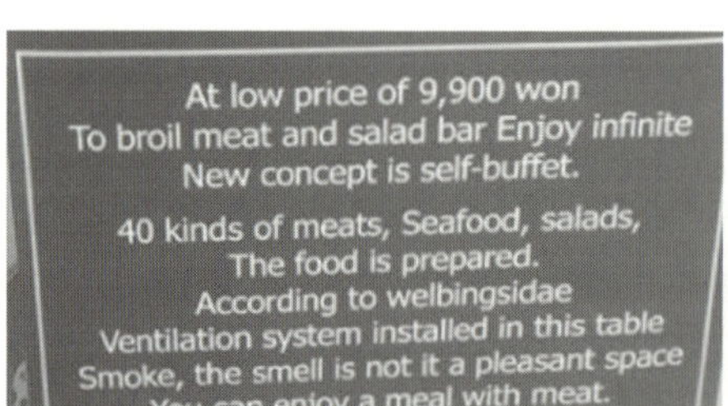

left image: [corrected version] "At the low price of 9,900 won, you can grill meat and enjoy an all-you-can-eat salad bar buffet. With 40 kinds of meats, seafood, and salads, the food is ready for you. For your well-being, all tables have a ventilation system installed that removes the smoke allowing you to enjoy a meal with meat."
right image: [corrected version] "I love dogs."

Conversations

Conversation: Distribution Channels

1. What are the four basic parts of a supply chain?
   a) The four parts of the supply chain are the manufacturer, wholesaler, retailer, and consumer.
   b) A distribution channel is made up of the manufacturer, wholesaler, retailer, and consumer.

2. What do you think is the most important part of the supply chain?
   a) The most important part of the supply chain is the consumer because that is where all of the power is.
   b) The most important part of the supply chain is the manufacturer because without them, we would not have any products to buy.

3. Do you think real estate agents are useful?
   a) No, they aren't. Real estate agents are just middlemen who get money for doing just a little work. I'd rather buy directly from the owner.
   b) Yes, they are. They know a lot about the real estate laws. They can help me buy an apartment easily.

4. Have you ever used a travel agent?
   a) Yes, I have. I used a travel agent before I went to Europe. They got a discount on a package tour for me.
   b) No, I haven't. I went abroad, but I didn't need an agent to help me. I just bought the tickets online by myself.

5. Why are small shops more expensive than big retail stores?
   a) Small shops don't have many products, so they have to be expensive to make a profit.
   b) Big retail stores have a well-organized supply chain. They can get discounts by ordering many products at once.

6. Do you think "the customer is always right"?
   a) Yes, I do. The customer is the most important part of the supply chain. Without the customer, the store will fail.
   b) No, I don't. Customers should respect the store's policies too. Sometimes, the customer can be wrong.

7. What is your favorite retail store?
   a) My favorite retail store is a Nike specialty shop. It carries many good Nike products, and I can find the latest fashions there.
   b) My favorite retail store is E–mart. It has many kinds of products, and I can always find something I need there.

8. How does Dunkin' Donuts get fresh donuts every day?
   a) I think Dunkin' Donuts makes all of their donuts nearby, and they are delivered by truck in the morning.
   b) Dunkin' Donuts has a fast delivery service that delivers to every store every morning, so the donuts are always fresh.

9. Why do many manufacturers move to China?
   a) It is very cheap to build factories in China because China is very large. Korea is a small country, so land is expensive.
   b) Labor costs in China are very cheap. A Chinese worker will earn only a little money, but Koreans usually earn a lot of money doing the same job.

10. What is your favorite restaurant franchise?
    a) My favorite franchise is Domino Pizza. I think their pizza is the best in Korea, and I usually order from that pizza restaurant.
    b) My favorite franchise is Lotteria. Their food is much better than McDonald's, and I really like hamburgers.

11. Have you ever purchased plane tickets online?
    a) No, I haven't. I've never been abroad, so I've never purchased any plane tickets online.
    b) Yes, I have. I usually use Travelocity.com to buy my plane tickets. They have great discount prices.

12. Why do some people buy tickets online instead of at a travel agency?
    a) People usually buy tickets online because it is much easier than buying from a travel agency.
    b) I think people buy tickets online because the tickets are a lot cheaper than at the airport.

13. Would you consider buying a car on the Internet?
    a) No, I wouldn't. I never trust online companies, especially with a big purchase decision like a car.
    b) Yes, I would. If I find a really good deal, it might be best to buy a car online. The Internet always has the best deals.

14. Why is the Korean postal delivery service ("Tekbae") so fast?
    a) Korea is a very small country, so the delivery service only takes a day or two to deliver any product anywhere.
    b) Koreans are very hard workers and work very efficiently. They do not waste any time when delivering products.

15. Are there any manufacturing companies in Busan?

16. Where are big ships built in Korea?

17. Where can you buy a screw driver? some paper? a new computer?

18. Do you ever buy foreign products?

19. Why is Busan famous for fresh fish?

20. What is your favorite kind of soju, and where is it made?

Part II

Today's Idiom

"... to get away with it..."

(ex. "He got away with murder.")

Pronunciation

/U/: Book

To make the /U/ sound, you just make the /u/ sound but relax your lips. You can combine this sound to make the /w/ sound, such as in 'wolf' or 'would'.

Beginning	Middle	End
-	book	-
-	nook	-
-	would	-
-	foot	-
-	should	-
-	put	-

1. He took a look at the good cookbook.
2. Ariel would like to put her foot on the wooden box.
3. I should hang my wool coat on the hook.
4. In the chess game, he could have used his rook.
5. God forsook Israel because they wouldn't obey to his holy book.
6. The dog shook after swimming in the brook.

Drills

Drill #1: Substitution

(possessive pronouns)

Key	Answer
This is a computer. – mine	*This computer is mine.*
your	*This is your computer.*
hers	*This computer is hers.*

Key	Answer
1. his computer	This … his computer.
2. her car	… her car.
3. mine	This car … mine.
4. yours	… yours.
5. our	This is our ...
6. my job	… job.
7. theirs	This job … theirs.
8. hers	This job is ...
9. her	… her job.
10. is his	This job ...
11. ours	This job ....
12. their desk	… their desk.
13. theirs	This … theirs.
14. yours	This … yours.
15. your	This ...
16. mine	This ...
17. hers	...
18. our	...
19. her	...
20. his	...

Drill #2: Q&A

(contrary adjectives)

Key	Answer
The cat - fat ---	*Is the cat fat?* *No, it isn't a fat cat. It's a thin cat.*
Kang, Ho-dong well-known comedian ---	*Is Kang, Ho-dong a well-known comedian?* *No, he isn't a well-known comedian. He is an unknown comedian.*

1. this supermarket - cheap **2. ---**	Is this … cheap? No, It isn't a cheap supermarket. It's an expensive ….
3. this gas range - dangerous **4. ---**	Is … dangerous? No, It isn't a dangerous … safe ...
5. the girl - tall **6. ---**	… girl tall? No, she isn't a … a short girl.
7. this bag - heavy **8. ---**	Is …? No, it isn't ... It's … light ....
9. these - strong windows **10. ---**	Are these strong …? No, they ... They're weak ...
11. the teacher - strict **12. ---**	… strict? … a lenient teacher.
13. the kids - good **14. ---**	…? …
15. he - mean clerk **16. ---**	… …
17. the water - hot **18. ---**	…? …
19. it - dirty room **20. ---**	…? …

Conversations

Conversation: Communication

1. How many text messages do you send every day?
   a) I send around 15 text messages every day because I like to talk to my friends.
   b) I usually don't send any text messages because I usually communicate through the Internet.

2. How do you usually contact your friends?
   a) I contact my friends through Facebook. It is very convenient and easy to use.
   b) I usually just send a text message or give my friends a call to keep in touch.

3. Do you use any social networking sites?
   a) No, I don't. These days, I don't use any social networking sites because I am busy.
   b) Yes, I do. I use Facebook. It is very popular among university students.

4. Do you think alcohol helps people communicate better?
   a) No, I don't. Alcohol makes people dizzy and confused, so I don't think it helps them communicate better.
   b) Yes, I do. Alcohol helps nervous people to relax and reduces stress, so people who drink can communicate more easily.

5. Do you prefer to communicate with email or by phone call?
   a) I prefer to call people when I have to talk about something important.
   b) I like sending an email rather than calling somebody since it is more convenient for both of us.

6. When you call someone, do you call via home phone or cell phone?
   a) I always call via my cell phone. The cell phone bills are not expensive if the call is short.
   b) I like to call someone with my home phone if it is local. The home phone is cheaper than using a cell phone.

7. Do you think the Internet is damaging social relationships?
   a) Yes, I do. These days, people spend too much time online and do not socialize.
   b) No, I don't. The Internet helps people communicate more because of social networking sites and messenger systems.

8. Who do you contact when you have a problem with a product?
   a) When I have a problem with a product, I usually go to the service center to fix it.
   b) I call the company to explain my problem and ask about a solution.

9. Where can you ask questions about a new product?
   a) You can ask questions about new products on brand websites, such as the brand's Facebook group page.
   b) You can go to the store where you bought the product and ask the salespeople for help.

10. Can you keep secrets well?
    a) Yes, I can. I never tell a person's secrets to other people. Secrets are important.
    b) No, I can't. I don't like to know secrets because I always think about them.

11. Can you communicate effectively in English?
    a) No, I can't. English is very difficult to use, but I am improving.
    b) Yes, I can. I can speak English pretty well. I have studied English for many years.

12. What topics do you enjoy talking about?
    a) I enjoy talking about sports, especially soccer. I always watch soccer on television.
    b) I like to talk about shopping. I love to go shopping and buy new things.

13. Do you use hand gestures when you are talking?
    a) No, I don't. I don't use many hand gestures when I am talking because I am shy.
    b) Yes, I do. I always use hand gestures to add emphasis to my words.

14. Who do you prefer to confide in; your mother, father, or another person?
    a) I usually confide in my mother because she loves me very much.
    b) I almost always confide in my best friend. He gives great advice.

15. Do you feel comfortable giving a speech in front of people?
    a) Yes, I do. I have practiced giving a speech many times in front of people.
    b) No, I don't. Giving a speech with an audience always makes me nervous.

16. What are some things you should not talk about with a co-worker?

17. What are some good ways to make new friends?

18. Do you often talk to your classmates?

19. Why do people use Facebook so much to communicate?

20. How is communication helpful in the workplace?

Extra practice:

- Review the previous questions with your group, or ask new questions.
- Why are "middlemen" in a supply chain important?
- Why do some manufacturers open their own retail stores?
- What are some ways to communicate that you frequently use?

Lesson 14

Pronunciation

Part Ⅰ : /u/ & /U/

Part Ⅱ : / i /

Drills

Part Ⅰ : Article – Amazon.com cuts down on packaging

Tag Questions – adding a tag question for confirmation

Part Ⅱ : Q&A – Why did you... / Because...

Q&A – perfect tense – "Have you ever..."

Conversations

Part Ⅰ : Advertising I

Part Ⅱ : "Have you ever... " with free responses

Part I

Today's Proverb

"Give a man a fish and you feed him for a day; teach a man to fish and you feed him for a lifetime."

Pronunciation

/u/&/U/: Luke-Look

A review of /u/ and /U/.

Beginning	Middle	End
-	Luke - look	-
-	suit - soot	-
-	fool - full	-
-	pool - pull	-
-	stewed - stood	-
-	who'd - hood	-

1. Look, Luke, at the fool in the hood by the pool.
2. You'll find the book by his foot covered in soot.
3. You should wear a suit for the interview.
4. It's true that cooking food can make you full.
5. The rule could be changed soon.
6. Who should pull the rude man away?

Drills

Drill #1: Article

Amazon.com cuts down on packaging

(source: www.amazon.com)

In the end of 2013, Amazon.com declared that it would be undertaking its "Frustration–Free Packaging" plan. Since its beginning, Amazon has had trouble with consumers experiencing "wrap rage" and becoming frustrated in attempts to open packages from the company. The new packaging initiative aims to use smaller packages that are easier to open and made from recyclable cardboard materials. Amazon also seeks to reduce the overall amount of material used in packaging.

"We've all experienced the frustration of trying to remove a product from nearly impenetrable packaging like plastic clamshell cases and products bound by dozens of wire ties," said Jeff Bezos, founder and CEO of Amazon.com. "We've worked with both manufacturers and customers to design Frustration–Free Packaging that is easy–to–open, protects the product, and reduces waste. We now have more than 2,000 manufacturers in the program."

Amazon.com, a Seattle–based company, is continuing to coordinate with other members of its supply chain in hopes of saving the customers' time and money while providing more environmentally friendly packaging options.

Discussion Questions:

1. What's wrong with packaging these days?
2. What has Amazon.com started doing?
3. What's the goal of the new packaging?

4. Do you think packaging is important? Why or why not?
5. What is Amazon.com? Does Korea have an online shopping site like Amazon?
6. Do you ever buy products on the Internet?

Drill #2: Tag Questions

(adding a tag question for confirmation)

Key	Answer
You have a car.	*You have a car, don't you?*
He's a nice guy.	*He's a nice guy, isn't he?*
We needed a hard test	*We needed a hard test, didn't we?*
John won't come to school tomorrow.	*John won't come to school tomorrow, will he?*

1. I'm a great artist.	..., aren't I?
2. You're not a friendly person.	..., are you?
3. We didn't call our professor.	..., did we?
4. We never forget our books.	..., do we?
5. He said something bad.	..., didn't he?
6. Heather is a beautiful girl.	..., isn't she?
7. They'll be late for the dance.	..., won't they?
8. She didn't go to the night club.	..., did she?
9. We're going to go to the movie.	..., aren't we?
10. You ate supper.	..., didn't you?
11. Jerry finished the paper.	..., didn't he?
12. You'll call your mother.	..., won't you?
13. Sarah isn't angry.	..., is she?
14. I wasn't drunk last night.	..., was I?
15. She was happy on her birthday.	..., wasn't she?
16. It's cold today.	..., isn't it?
17. The weather was rainy yesterday.	..., wasn't it?
18. You heard me.	..., didn't you?
19. William is a Trade major.	..., isn't he?
20. Jenny doesn't speak English.	..., does she?

Conversations

Conversation: Advertising I

1. What's your favorite commercial?
   a) My favorite commercial is the Coke commercial with the polar bears.
   b) I don't have a favorite commercial because I don't usually watch television.

2. Where do you usually see advertisements?
   a) I usually see advertisements on the subway.
   b) I often watch TV, and there are many commercials between shows.

3. How do you learn about new products?
   a) I usually learn about new products when I surf the Internet.
   b) My friends usually tell me about new products that are good to buy.

4. Do you like to try free samples?
   a) Yes, I love trying free samples. They give me a good idea about the product's quality.
   b) No, I don't. Free samples are usually too small for me to know if the product is good or not.

5. What advertisement style do you like most?
   a) My favorite type of advertisement is interactive ads on the Internet. I like to play mini-games and learn about new products online.
   b) I usually enjoy TV commercials because they are always new and unique.

6. Do you think TV commercials are interesting?
   a) Yes, I do. TV commercials give me a good chance to catch up on new product information.
   b) No, I don't. I just want to watch a TV program. I don't want to watch commercials.

7. Do you read advertisements on the subway?
   a) No, I don't. I usually just stare at people on the subway.
   b) Yes, I do. I like to look at the pictures on the subway walls while I'm waiting for my stop.

8. How often do you take flyers from people on the street?
   a) I almost never take flyers from people on the street. They are just trash anyway.
   b) I always take flyers when people hand them out. It's their job, so I have to accept them.

9. Do you have any mileage cards?
   a) No, I don't. My girlfriend has mileage cards, but I don't have any.
   b) Yes, I do. I have a TGI Friday's Cajun Club card and a Dunkin' Donuts Happy Point card.

10. Which company advertises the most in Korea?
   a) I always see commercials on TV for Samsung products.
   b) LG advertises a lot in the subway and on the radio, so I think they advertise most in Korea.

11. Why do Korean supermarkets have a lot of people selling things in each aisle?
   a) Koreans like to learn about new products in the store. So, if somebody has a question, they can easily ask the salesperson.
   b) People might steal something if there isn't a person in the aisle watching carefully.

12. Do you ever click on banner ads while surfing the Internet?
   a) Yes, I do. I click on banner ads when they catch my eye.
   b) No, I don't. I almost never click on banner ads while surfing the Internet. I hate pop-ups too.

13. Do you think salespeople lie?
    a) Yes, I do. I can't trust some one who is trying to sell me something to make money.
    b) No, I don't, but I'm always very careful about where I buy something.

14. Do you trust commercials on TV?
    a) Yes, I do. Commercials usually give accurate information about a product.
    b) No, I don't. Commercials can't be trusted because they are biased.

15. How do you feel about salespeople on the subway?
    a) I think those people need to make money, so I don't mind them.
    b) They are so noisy, so I'm very irritated when they try to sell something.

*** Ask your partner 16-20, then switch and review. ***

16. What company do you want to work for?

17. How did you learn about that company?

18. Where can you see an advertisement for that company?

19. What kind of products or services does the company have?

20. Why do you think that company is good?

Part Ⅱ

Today's Idiom

Normal Expression: "Cat got your tongue?"

Correct Grammer: "Does the cat have your tongue?"

Pronunciation

/i/: Interest

To make the /i/ sound, you put the sides of your tongue up to touch your teeth and relax the middle with the tip of your tongue in a relaxed position.

Beginning	Middle	End
interest	slip	-
inside	tip	-
it	city	-
if	bill	-
itch	until	-
important	middle	-

1. I think paying the bill is in your best interest.
2. Will you tip the waiter with a five dollar bill?
3. It's important to carefully check your bill to see if there are any mistakes.
4. If you scratch the itch, it will feel better.
5. I tried not to slip on the thin patch of ice.
6. I left your lipstick inside your car.

Drills

Drill #1: Q&A Drill

(Why did you...? / Because...)

Key	Answer
I called my friend yesterday because I wanted to talk to him.	*A: Why did you call your friend?* *B: Because I wanted to talk to him.*
I left early because I didn't want to be late.	*A: Why did you leave early?* *B: Because I didn't want to be late*

1. I went to school because I wanted to learn something.	A: Why did ... go to school? B: Because I ...
2. I needed to buy some food because I was hungry.	A: Why ... need to ... food? B: ...
3. I didn't call my mother because I knew she wasn't home.	A: Why didn't ...? B: ...
4. I didn't pay the bill because I don't have my wallet.	A: Why didn't ...? B: ...
5. I helped her today because her job is difficult.	A: ...? B: ...
6. I felt sleepy today because I didn't sleep last night.	A: ...? B: ...
7. I didn't drive my car because I don't have any gas.	A: ...? B: ...
8. I didn't check my email because my computer is broken.	A: ...? B: ...
9. I finished my homework because I had some free time.	A: ...? B: ...
10. I brought my umbrella because it's going to rain.	A: ...? B: ...

Drill #2: Q&A Drill

(perfect tense - Have you ever...?)

Key	Answer
go, school	*Have you ever gone to school?*
(free response)	*Yes, I have.*
eat, dog	*Have you ever eaten dog?*
(free response)	*No, I haven't.*
1. take, trip	Have you ever taken a ...?
2. see, movie	... ever seen a ...?
3. spoke, French	... spoken French?
4. fight, with, friend	... fought with a friend?
5. go, abroad	... gone ...?
6. meet, famous person	... met a ...?
7. be, successful	...?
8. wear, contacts	...?
9. sing, rock and roll songs	...?
10. make, kimchi	...?

Conversations

Conversation: "Have you ever…" with Free Responses

*** Please explain your answer. ***

1. Have you ever been to another country?
2. Have you ever flown in an airplane?
3. Have you ever broken up with someone you loved?
4. Have you ever argued with your parents?
5. Have you ever eaten Mexican food?
6. Have you ever done any martial arts, such as Hapkido?
7. Have you ever tripped and fallen down stairs?
8. Have you ever thrown a punch at someone?

9. Have you ever gotten a bloody nose?
10. Have you ever been on a ship?
11. Have you ever done something really embarrassing?
12. Have you ever lost something you treasured?
13. Have you ever bought food but discovered you had no money?
14. Have you ever drank too much alcohol?
15. Have you ever stayed up all night long?
16. Have you ever given money to charity?
17. Have you ever been in a car accident?
18. Have you ever had to have surgery?
19. Have you ever made somebody really mad at you?
20. Have you ever worked for a good company?

Extra Practice:

– Review some of the previous questions

– Ask some more "Have you ever…" questions to your group.

– Why is international marketing important for companies?

– Which style of advertising is most effective for selling the following:

- Cars
- Snacks
- Music CDs
- Computers
- House cleaning services
- Tutoring services
- Gumo Apartments or Houses
- Clothes
- Fast Food

Lesson 15

Pronunciation

Part Ⅰ : /kw/

Part Ⅱ : /k/

Drills

Part Ⅰ : Sentence Transformation – phrasal verbs + pronouns
Response – more phrasal verbs + pronouns

Part Ⅱ : Interview and Free Response – sequencing words
Q&A – "wh-" questions + free response

Conversations

Part Ⅰ : Advertising Ⅱ

Part Ⅱ : Beauty

Part I

Today's Proverb

"That's the way the cookie crumbles."

Pronunciation

/kw/: Quit

To make the /kw/ sound, you simply combine the /k/ with a /w/. It is important to move your lips from a small /o/ to a relaxed form to get the proper sound of /w/.

Beginning	Middle	End
quit	aqua	-
quiet	squander	-
quite	square	-
queen	squirt	-
quota	squeamish	-
quote	require	-

1. I had a quiet meal after I quit my job.
2. Don't squirt the man with aquarium water.
3. Mozart is quite famous for his requiem.
4. I must request that you fill the quota.
5. My professor required a quote from Mark Twain.
6. The queen gave the squire a square piece of cheese.

Drills

Drill #1: Sentence Transformation

(phrasal verbs with pronouns)

Key	Answer
You need to do your report over.	*You need to do it over.*
I turned off the alarm.	*I turned it off.*
Sally put off her meeting.	*She put it off.*

Key	Answer
1. I called off the game.	I called it off.
2. He took over the team.	He took it over.
3. I looked over his essay.	I …it over.
4. The robber gave up the gun.	… gave it up.
5. Jerry took off his jacket.	… took … off.
6. Mina put on her makeup.	Mina put it ...
7. We gave back the library books.	We … them ...
8. They sorted out the problems.	…sorted them ...
9. Wanda put away her pencil.	… away.
10. Henry read up on Korean history.	…read up on it.
11. Lisa got through with her work.	… through with it.
12. Jason cleaned up the spill.	… cleaned it up.
13. Sarah and I tossed around the ball.	… it around.
14. Julie and Liz cheered up their sad friend.	… her up.
15. The tornado blew over the sign.	… blew it ...

Drill #2: Response

(more phrasal verbs and Drill #1 review)

Key	Answer
Did you do your homework over?	*Yes, I did it over.*
Did you get over your cold?	*Yes, I got over it.*
Did you get through with your work?	*Yes, I got through with it.*

1. Did he call off the game?	Yes, he ...
2. Did the professor look over your essay?	Yes, he ...
3. Did Jane toss around the baseball?	Yes, she tossed it around.
4. Did the typhoon blow over the sign?	Yes, it ...
5. Did they clean up the spill?	Yes, they … it up.
6. Did they turn in their homework?	Yes, … it in.
7. Did they sort out the problem?	.. they sorted it ...
8. Did she read up on Korean history?	… read up on it.
9. Did you catch up to Sally yesterday?	… caught up to ...
10. Did the robber give up the gun?	.. gave it up.

Conversations

Conversation: Advertising Ⅱ

1. What's your favorite brand?
   a) My favorite brand is LG because they make great electronics.
   b) I really like Coca-Cola because it is fun to drink.

2. Where do you usually see your favorite brand?
   a) I usually see advertisements for it on the subway.
   b) I often see my favorite brand in the supermarket.

3. How do you learn about new services?
   a) I usually learn about new services when I shop in a store.
   b) My friends usually tell me about new services that they have experienced.

4. Do you like to try new products?
   a) Yes, I love trying new products. I always want to be the first to buy something good.
   b) No, I don't. New products are not always good quality, so I like to listen to others' opinions first.

5. What advertisement style do you like most?
   a) My favorite type of advertisement is interactive ads on the Internet. I like to play mini-games and learn about new products online.
   b) I usually enjoy TV commercials because they are always new and unique.

6. Do you think subway ads are interesting?
   a) Yes, I do. Subway ads give me a good chance to catch up on new product information.
   b) No, I don't. I usually don't even look at the ads on the subway walls.

7. Do you read advertisements in magazines?
   a) No, I don't. I usually just read the articles.
   b) Yes, I do. I like to look at the pictures in the magazines and see what's new.

8. How often do you try free samples?
   a) I almost never try free samples. I usually just buy the product.
   b) I always try free samples. They help me choose the best product.

9. Do you have any coupons right now?
   a) No, I don't. My girlfriend has some coupons in her purse, but I don't have any.
   b) Yes, I do. I have a coupon for a free hamburger at McDonald's.

10. Which company advertises the most in the world?
   a) I always see commercials on TV for Coca-cola.
   b) Obviously, McDonald's is the company that advertises the most. Its ads are everywhere.

11. Do you prefer to talk to a salesperson or shop without help?
    a) I like to shop without help. Salespeople are too pushy.
    b) I enjoy talking to salespeople about products because they are knowledgeable about them.

12. Do you ever visit online shopping malls?
    a) Yes, I do. I often buy food from online grocery stores.
    b) I don't usually buy anything online, but I like to browse the shopping malls.

13. Do you think salespeople are trustworthy?
    a) No, I don't. I can't trust some one who is trying to sell me something to make money.
    b) Yes, I do, but I'm always very careful about where I buy something.

14. Do you trust infomercials on TV?

15. How do you feel about salespeople on the street?

*** Ask your partner 16-20, then switch and repeat. ***

16. What product do you want to buy?

17. How did you learn about that product?

18. Where can you see an advertisement for that product?

19. What kind of features or attributes does that product have?

20. Why do you think that product is good?

Part Ⅱ

Today's Idiom

"Better luck next time."

Pronunciation

/k/: Keep

To make the /k/ sound, you must put the back part of your tongue against the roof of your mouth and drop it down while letting air pass over it. Notice the middle and end /k/ is often softer than the beginning /k/.

Beginning	Middle	End
keep	taking	took
kit	asked	flask
kosher	victory	bike
culminate	occupation	ask
corrupt	accumulate	fork
care	hiking	forsake

1. Do not forsake the president even if he is corrupt.
2. I don't care for hiking because I like biking.
3. Keep your hands to yourself.
4. Ask Ken if he only eats kosher or if pork is ok.
5. After college, finding an occupation is important.
6. Don't drink and take a car out for a spin.

Drills

Drill #1: Interview and Free Response

(sequencing words – first, then, after that, next, and then, finally)

Key	Answer
What did you do today?	*First, I got out of bed.* *And then, I washed my face.* *Next, I ate breakfast,* *After that, I brushed my teeth.* *Then, I took the bus to school.* *Finally, I arrived at class.*

1. What did you do yesterday? **2. What will you do this week?** **3. What do you do on Mondays?**	**4. What will you do tomorrow?** **5. What did you do last weekend?** **6. What do you do on Saturday night?**

Drill #2: Question and Free Response

(who, what, where, when, why)

Key	Answer
where, going ***(free response)***	*Where are you going?* *(free response) I'm going to class*
what, doing ***(free response)***	*What are you doing?* *I am studying English.*

1. Who, did, come, school, with	...
2. Why, study, English	...
3. What, favorite, food	...
4. Where, do, do, your, homework	...
5. Why, did, skip, lunch	...
6. What, this	...
7. When, call, your, mother	...
8. Who, best, friend	...

9. What, favorite, color	…
10. Where, going, after, class	…
11. When, you, happy	…
12. Why, did, wear, coat	…
13. Where, do, keep, your, books	…
14. Who, did, eat, breakfast, with	…
15. Why, did, go, bed, late, last night	…

Conversations

Conversation: Beauty

1. Who is the most beautiful person in Korea?
    a) I think Hye Gyo Song is the most beautiful actress in Korea.
    b) Wow, I think Hyori Lee is so beautiful. She is really fashionable and attractive.

2. Do you think beauty helps people succeed?
    a) Yes, I do. Beautiful people are often very successful.
    b) No, I don't. Talent is more important than beauty in the world today.

3. How much time do you spend in front of a mirror in the morning?
    a) I spend about 10 minutes in front of the mirror in the morning to wash my face.
    b) I need about 30 minutes in front of the mirror every day to put on my makeup.

4. Do you think it's ok for men to wear makeup?
    a) Yes, I do. Japanese men wear makeup, and they look great.
    b) No, I don't. I think only women should wear makeup.

5. What are some tips to keep our skin looking young?
    a) I think not smoking is the most important way to keep our skin young.
    b) Wearing lotion every day and every night is the best way to protect our skin.

6. How do you feel about tattoos?
   a) Tattoos are only for gangsters. I would never get a tattoo!
   b) I think tattoos are interesting. I would like to get one.

7. Is it ok for men to wear earrings?
   a) Yes, it is. Many men wear earrings these days, and it's very fashionable.
   b) No, it isn't. Men shouldn't wear earrings, makeup, or miniskirts.

8. What is your ideal type physically?
   a) I like tall men with many muscles and good fashion.
   b) I love short girls with long hair and long eyelashes.

9. What do you think about plastic surgery?
   a) I really like plastic surgery. I want to get plastic surgery to change my nose. My nose is too big.
   b) I don't like plastic surgery. I think natural beauty is more important.

10. What are some problems with being attractive?
    a) I can't think of any problems with being attractive.
    b) Attractive women have to be careful on the subway and at night. There are many bad men in the city.

11. How do you feel when someone stares at you?
    a) I really hate it when somebody stares at me. It makes me uncomfortable.
    b) I don't care when someone stares at me. They can look, but they can't touch.

12. Do you use regular soap in the shower or a body wash?
    a) I usually use a body wash in the shower. It doesn't dry out my skin.
    b) I just use regular soap in the shower. I think soap is good for getting my skin clean.

13. Which is better, being really smart or being really attractive?
    a) Being really smart is important because without a good mind, you will fail many times in your life.
    b) I think being really attractive is better because attractive people are often more successful and famous than smart people.

14. Do you worry about getting older?
    a) Yes, I do. I am afraid of losing my good looks with age.
    b) No, I don't. After I'm married, I don't have to worry about my appearance as much.

15. Do you spend a lot of money on beauty or skin-care products?
    a) Yes, I do. I spend over 100,000 won a month on makeup.
    b) No, I don't. I just buy cheap lotion every now and then.

16. What do you think "beauty is only skin deep" means?

17. What is "inner beauty"?

18. Do you think your mother is beautiful and your father is handsome?

19. Is it ok for children to be obsessed with physical appearance?

20. What do you want to change about your appearance?

Extra Practice:

- Review some of the previous questions.
- Tell about your day. Make sentences using first, then, next, and then, after that, and finally.
- Why do Korean companies usually require a picture on a resume?
- What do guys and girls do differently when they get ready for going on a date?
- What do you think of a woman wearing perfume or a man wearing cologne?
- What is the most beautiful place in Korea?

Lesson 16

Pronunciation

Part I : /ah/

Part II : /aw/

Drills

Part I : Q&A – "to like" & "to be like" review and free response

Dialogue – Selling an Audio System

Part II : Q&A – tag questions + short answer

Article – A Memo from the Service Center

Conversations

Part I : Products and Features

Part II : Home

Part I

Today's Proverb

"Actions speak louder than words."

Pronunciation

/ah/: Opposite

The /ah/ sound is the exact same sound as the Korean /ah/ sound. Most mistakes for Koreans come from pronunciation of the words like 'modern' and 'model'.

Beginning	Middle	End
opposite	father	-
opera	botch	-
odd	cop	-
operation	lollipop	-
opportunity	helicopter	-
ouch	model	-

1. Opera singers practice singing "do re mi fa so la ti do".
2. It's odd to think that your father is a cop.
3. Don't spill the pop on top of your lollipop.
4. He stopped the operator from botching the opportunity.
5. The crops were ruined when the helicopter dropped the box.

Drills

Drill #1: Q&A – Two Uses of "Like" [a review of Lesson 3] and Free Response

(What do you like? / What are you like?)

Key	Answer
What do you like?	*(Free Response) I like apples and oranges.*
What are you like?	*(Free Response) I am a nice and smart person.*
What is your apartment like?	*(Free Response) It is on the 6th floor, and it is small.*

1. What is your partner like?	**9. What does your best friend like?**
2. What does your partner like?	**10. What are your sunglasses like?**
3. What is your TV like?	**11. What are you like?**
4. What are your classmates like?	**12. What do you like?**
5. What do your classmates like?	**13. What is that person like?**
6. What does your father like?	**14. What do those people like?**
7. What is your school like?	**15. What are your weekends like?**
8. What is your neighborhood like?	**16. What do Koreans like?**

Drill #2: Dialogue

(Selling an Audio System)

Salesperson: "Good morning, sir. Can I help you with anything today?"

Customer: "Yes, I'm interested in a home theater system for under 1,000 dollars. Do you happen to have any in-stock at the moment?"

Salesperson: "Yes, sir, we do have a complete surround sound home theater system in stock. It is made by Infinity, which is a very famous company for good quality sound."

Customer: "I see. So, how much is the entire system?"

Salesperson: "The Infinity Total Solutions Home Theater System costs 899 dollars before tax. If you purchase the system today, there is a

10% discount on the price."

Customer: "Wow, that's a great discount! Why is there 10% off only today?"

Salesperson: "Today is the last day that this system is on sale. Tomorrow, the system will be at the regular price again."

Customer: "Well, I will definitely buy it today. I don't want to miss the boat on this one. I've got cash, so let's go to the register, and you can ring me up."

Conversations

Conversation: Products and Features

1. What kind of car do you want to buy?
   a) I want to buy a sports car because I like speed.
   b) I would like to buy an economical car. Gasoline is too expensive these days.

2. What feature is most important when buying a car?
   a) The most important feature when buying a car is safety. I want my family to be safe.
   b) I think good gas mileage is the most important feature for a car. Gas is pricey.

3. What is the best feature on your cell phone?
   a) The DMB function is the best feature on my cell phone. I always watch TV on the bus with it.
   b) The best feature on my cell phone is the high quality camera. I like to take pictures and post them on my Facebook page.

4. What is the most useless feature on your cell phone?
   a) I never use the Blue Tooth option. It is the most useless feature.
   b) I never listen to any music on my cell phone. The MP3 feature is the most useless for me.

5. What kind of computer do you have?
   a) I have a Samsung computer. It is new and very fast.
   b) I have an LG computer. It's old, but it still runs well enough for me.

6. Do you think your computer is too old? Why or why not?
   a) No, I don't. I can surf the Internet and watch movies without any lag.
   b) Yes, I do. I can't play the latest games on my old computer because it's too slow.

7. What feature is important when buying an umbrella?
   a) I think low price is the most important feature for an umbrella.
   b) I want to buy an umbrella that is durable and will last a really long time.

8. What is the most important thing to consider when buying groceries?
   a) I want to buy cheap groceries, so I always look for the cheapest place to shop.
   b) Selection is the most important thing to consider. When I buy groceries, I want to have many choices.

9. What do you like most about your apartment?
   a) I like my apartment because it is really big. We have 4 bedrooms and 2 bathrooms.
   b) Actually, I live in the dormitory. It is close to the university, so it only takes 5 minutes to come here on foot.

10. What needs to be repaired or remodeled in your apartment?
    a) My sink is leaking, so I need to call a plumber to come fix it.
    b) I really want to get new wallpaper. The wallpaper is old and looks bad.

11. What should you consider when shopping for a gift?
    a) I think trying to find a fun gift is important. I want to give a gift that is memorable and enjoyable.
    b) You really should consider a useful gift. If you can eat it or use it, then it is a good gift.

12. Why do some people buy used cars instead of new cars?
    a) People buy used cars because they want to save money. New cars are too expensive.
    b) I think people buy used cars because having a new car is stressful. If my new car gets scratched, I will probably go out of my mind.

13. Do you mind getting hand-me-downs from your family?
    a) No, I don't. I like to wear my older brother's old clothes, so I don't have to always buy new ones.
    b) Yes, I do. I don't want to wear old clothes or shoes that my family wore before.

14. How often do you buy new clothes?
    a) I buy a new piece of clothing at least once a week.
    b) I might buy something new to wear once or twice a month.

15. What are some of the features on your television?

16. Do you have a dictionary application on your cell phone?

17. What do you want to buy soon?

18. Where can you buy the best Samsung products?

19. What stores have the largest selection of goods?

20. Tell me about your favorite tech gadget?

Part Ⅱ

Today's Idiom

"... a snowball effect." or "...to snowball."
(ex. "Lately, my problems have snowballed.")

Pronunciation

/aw/: Office

To make the /aw/ sound, just relax your tongue and use your voice. In Korean the /aw/ sound is the dark vowel opposite of /ah/.

Beginning	Middle	End
office	taught	law
ought	wroth	maw
authorize	lawn	gnaw
awe	wrong	straw
art	yawn	flaw
alms	wall	raw

1. Almost all Koreans like to eat raw fish.
2. Turn off the light just like I taught you.
3. The last straw was when he wronged me.
4. In the autumn, my mother-in-law mows the lawn.
5. He doesn't belong to the lost children of Austria.

Drills

Drill #1: Q&A

(tag questions with short answers)

Key	Answer
I can use your book.	*I can use your book, can't I?* *Yes, you can. / No, you can't.*
He is going to the movies.	*He is going to the movies, isn't he?* *Yes, he is. / No, he isn't.*

1. You will brush your teeth.	..., won't you?
2. You called your mother.	..., didn't you
3. John wrote the address down.	..., didn't he?
4. Mary and I will work together.	..., won't we?
5. My professor forgets his book.	..., doesn't he?
6. The pen is on the desk.	..., isn't it?
7. The cars were repaired.	..., weren't they?
8. The secretary gave you a memo.	..., didn't she?
9. My girlfriend sent you an email.	..., didn't she?
10. Andy won't come to class.	..., will he?
11. I don't look healthy.	..., do I?
12. My kids are growing fast.	..., aren't they?
13. The answer isn't correct.	..., is it?
14. We haven't gotten back yet.	..., have we?
15. I study hard everyday.	..., don't I?
16. You couldn't open the door.	..., could you?
17. She can do the homework.	..., can't she?
18. I am happy.	..., aren't I? (..., am I not?)
19. She isn't angry.	..., is she?
20. They wouldn't have gone.	..., would they?

Drill #2: Article

A Memo from the Service Center

To: Angel Mist

From: Heidi Rain

Date: May 3rd

Subject: Service Report for Samsung PC

I have received your PC and investigated the problem that you reported. You stated that the computer was working fine last week, but on Monday, you lost the video. You also said that you thought that the problem may involve your graphics card.

I checked the graphics card by swapping out the old one and putting in a new card, but your computer did not boot. I also changed the power supply and tried to boot the system, and everything worked fine. I suspect your old power supply died and took out your video card with it. Sometimes, a dying power supply can cause a domino effect of failures on a computer. Anyway, the problem was hardware related and not your fault.

The computer is now working fine and is ready to be picked up at the service center whenever you have time. The charge for the repairs will be four hundred dollars.

Questions:

1. What did Ms. Mist say her computer's problem was?
2. What did Ms. Mist suspect caused the problem?
3. What did Ms. Rain do first and what was the result?
4. What did Ms. Rain do second and what was the result?
5. Why did the video card die?
6. What can a dying power supply do to a computer?
7. Was the problem Ms. Mist's fault?
8. Where can Ms. Mist pick up the computer?
9. How much was the service charge for the computer?

Extra:

- What does "swapping out" mean?
- What does "domino effect" mean?

Conversations

Conversation: Home

1. How many people live in your apartment?
    a) Two people live in my apartment; my mother and me.
    b) There are three people living in my apartment; my two roommates and me.

2. What is the cleanest room in your apartment?
    a) The cleanest room in my apartment is the bathroom. My mother always cleans it.
    b) The kitchen is the cleanest room in my apartment because I always clean it.

3. Do you have any pets?
   a) Yes, I do. I have a small dog. He is very cute.
   b) No, I don't. I don't really like pets because they are expensive.

4. What chores do you do?
   a) I usually wash dishes, sweep the floor, and take out the trash.
   b) I try to help my mother cook food once in a while.

5. What brand of refrigerator do you have?
   a) I have a Samsung Zippel refrigerator. It is very convenient to use.
   b) My family has an LG Dios. We bought it recently because our old one was broken.

6. Do you like your apartment?
   a) Yes, I do. My apartment is very comfortable and close to the subway.
   b) No, I don't. My apartment is too old and a little too small.

7. When did you move to your apartment?
   a) I moved to my apartment three years ago when I came to this university.
   b) I have lived in my current apartment since I was born.

8. How many apartments or houses have you lived in?
   a) I have moved six times in my life. My family often moved because of work.
   b) I haven't moved in my life. I have always lived in my current apartment.

9. Do you prefer to study at home or at school?
   a) I prefer to study at school because the library is a very good place to study.
   b) I prefer to study at home because it is more comfortable and quiet than school.

10. What do you usually do at home?
   a) I usually just sleep when I am at home. I am very tired these days.
   b) I often watch TV or play computer games at home because I have a lot of free time.

11. Is your apartment building old?
   a) No, it isn't. My apartment building is only a few years old. It is very modern.
   b) Yes, it is. My apartment is more than ten years old and always needs repair.

12. What time do you usually go home?
   a) I usually go home around 6pm every day.
   b) These days, I am busy, so I don't get home until after 10 pm.

13. How many computers do you have at home?
   a) My family has three computers at home; a desktop and two laptops.
   b) I have two computers at home; a tablet and a desktop.

14. Do you like to play music through speakers at home?
   a) Yes, I do. I often play music through my computer speakers when I am home alone.
   b) No, I don't. My neighborhood is very quiet, so I usually just use headphones.

15. How many bathrooms do you have in your apartment?
   a) I have only one bathroom in my apartment that my family shares.
   b) I have two bathrooms in my apartment. One is the main bathroom, and the other is in my parents' room.

16. How do you feel about home?

17. Do you have your own room or do you share with somebody?

18. Which is better, living on the top floor or the bottom floor?
19. What color are your bedroom walls?
20. Does your apartment have a good view?

Extra Practice:

- Review some of the previous questions.
- Tell about some products you bought recently.
- Where is your favorite place to shop for cosmetics or clothes?
- Why is a house better than an apartment? And, why is an apartment better than a house?
- Do you think your hometown is a safe place to live? Why or why not?

Lesson 17

Pronunciation

Part Ⅰ : /sh/

Part Ⅱ : /shz/

Drills

Part Ⅰ : Q&A – pronoun - one/it [a review of Lesson 9]

Q&A – pronoun - some/any/them [a review of Lesson 9]

Part Ⅱ : Tag Questions – review of Lesson 14

Q&A and Free Response – review of Lesson 16

Conversations

Part Ⅰ : The Internet and Online Shopping

Part Ⅱ : Community

Part I

Today's Proverb

"Money is the root of all evil." – [common misquote]

"The love of money is the root of all evil." (1 Timothy 6:10) – [original quote]

Pronunciation

/sh/: Shard

A review of /sh/ from Lesson 11.

Beginning	Middle	End
shard	fished	wash
shrill	dishes	trash
shrimp	pushed	English
shale	fraction	gnash
shirk	actually	clash
should	kosher	whiplash

1. Moshe (Moses) actually clashed with the pharaoh.
2. If you follow a kosher diet, you should not eat shrimp.
3. Shall we begin to share the fish just as Yeshua (Jesus) did?
4. Pushing your friend to study English is something she won't appreciate.
5. A fraction of the dish of fresh mashed potatoes was thrown in the trash.
6. When cars crash, you should be careful of whiplash.

[NOTE: "Moshe" and "Yeshua" are the Hebrew pronunciations of "Moses" and "Jesus."]

Drills

Drill #1: Q&A Drill

(pronouns - one/it) [a review of Lesson 9]

Key	Answer
sing - a song ***yes***	*Did you sing a song?* *Yes, I sang one.*
play - his piano ***no***	*Did you play his piano?* *No, I didn't play it.*
1. have - an apple **2. yes**	Did you have an …? Yes, … had one.
3. use - my computer **4. no**	Did you use my …? No, I … use it.
5. take - her book **6. yes**	Did you … her …? … took it.
7. see - the movie **8. no**	Did you …? No, I … it.
9. sell - a car **10. yes**	Did … car? … one.
11. use - the money **12. no**	.. you use …? No, I … it.
13. take - a shower **14. no**	Did …? No, … one.
15. fix - the pipe **16. yes**	…? … it.
17. take - a picture **18. no**	…? ...
19. watch - the game **20. yes**	…? ...

Drill #2: Q&A Drill

(pronouns - some/any/them) [a review of Lesson 9]

Key	Answer
Clean - socks ***yes***	*Did you clean socks?* *Yes, I cleaned some.*
Buy - the cakes ***no***	*Did you buy the cakes?* *No, I didn't buy them.*

1. sell - cars **2. yes**	Did you sell …? Yes, …sold some.
3. light - candles **4. no**	Did you …? No, I didn't … any.
5. spend - money **6. yes**	…spend any money? … spent some.
7. wear - your shoes **8. no**	Did …? No, I didn't … them.
9. have - tea **10. no**	Did … any tea? … any.
11. hug - your friends **12. yes**	… your friends? Yes, … them.
13. bring - some clothes **14. yes**	… some clothes? Yes, …
15. taste - the peaches **16. yes**	Did …? … them.
17. forget - your glasses **18. no**	Did …? ...
19. watch - movies **20. yes**	…? ...

Key word pronunciation

Internet, online, shop/shopping, products, www.naver.com, clothes, mall, expensive

Conversations

Conversation: The Internet and Online Shopping

1. Where is a good place to buy products online?
   a) I usually buy products from www.gmarket.co.kr.
   b) I usually just use naver.com to find products I want to buy.

2. Do you often buy products online?
   a) Yes, I do. I always buy clothes online.
   b) No, I don't, but I did buy a new computer mouse online one year ago.

3. What kinds of things are good to buy on the Internet?
   a) I think buying clothes on the Internet is cheap and fast.
   b) I don't know. I never really buy anything online.

4. What kinds of things are difficult to buy on the Internet?
   a) It is really difficult to buy furniture on the Internet. Shipping is too expensive.
   b) I don't think you can buy cigarettes or alcohol online, since children use the Internet.

5. Do you trust online shopping malls?
   a) Yes, I trust them. I have never had a bad experience shopping online.
   b) No, I don't trust them. I'm worried that they can steal my money or send me a bad product.

6. Have you ever bought something online that you didn't like?
   a) Yes, I have. I bought a shirt that was too small.
   b) No, I haven't. Everything I bought online was exactly what I expected.

7. Do you use Internet banking?

a) Yes, I do. I sometimes use Internet banking to send money to buy something online.

b) No, I don't. I just use an ATM to send money.

Online and mobile banking

% of internet users who do online banking vs. the % of cell phone owners who use mobile banking

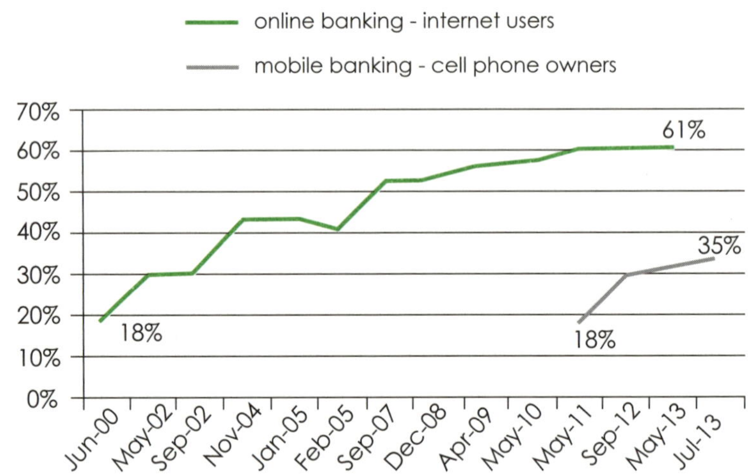

Source: Pew Research Center's Internet & American Life Trackign and Omnibus Surveys, 2000–2013. Margin of error for results based on internet users is +/–2.5 percentage points and +/–3.8 percentage points for results based on cell phone owners.

8. Are products more expensive on the Internet?

a) Of course not! Products are almost always cheaper online.

b) Yes, they sometimes are. Actually, they are cheaper, but after shipping costs, they are more expensive.

9. What do you usually use the Internet for?

a) I listen to songs on an Internet radio station, and I check the news daily.

b) I usually use the Internet to study and prepare for my classes.

10. How often do you use the Internet?
    a) I always use the Internet. I will use the Internet today when I go home.
    b) I sometimes use the Internet when I have free time.

11. How long do you spend on the Internet every day?
    a) I spend about 3 hours every day surfing the Internet.
    b) I am usually online for about 2 to 3 hours a week.

12. Do you take longer to shop in a store or to shop online?
    a) I take longer shopping in a store than online because I have to try on clothes and examine the products.
    b) Shopping online takes longer for me because I want to visit many sites before I buy a product.

13. Do you think that Internet shopping will become more popular in the future?
    a) Yes, I do. More people are using the Internet everyday, so I think it will become more popular.
    b) No, I don't. Shopping in stores is more fun, so I think people will only use the Internet when they are too busy.

14. What do you think of pop-up ads?
    a) I like them because they give me information about new sites and products.
    b) I hate them because they are always popping up when I'm trying to do something else.

15. Do you get a lot of spam mail advertisements?
    a) Yes, I do. My junk mailbox is full of spam mail every day.
    b) No, I don't. I usually don't get much spam mail.

16. Do you ever give your email address to companies?

17. What website do you visit the most?

18. Do you think it can be dangerous to meet people from the Internet?

19. What are some major advantages of the Internet?

20. What are some major disadvantages of the Internet?

Part II

Today's Idiom

"... the home stretch..."

(ex. "We're in the home stretch.")

Pronunciation

/shz/: Genre

The /shz/ sound is made simply by making an /sh/ sound and adding voice to it.

Beginning	Middle	End
genre	Asia	triage
-	casual	collage
-	treasure	prestige
-	occasion	beige
-	television	garage
-	lesion	mirage

1. What genre do you recommend for a casual television viewer?
2. She wore the corsage she received on the special occasion.
3. In America, people often hold garage sales to sell old treasures.
4. Prestige can sometimes vanish like a desert mirage.
5. Despite the protection of his entourage, Tupac was shot and experienced triage.
6. Asian scientists are researching cold fusion.

Drills

Drill #1: Tag Questions

(a review of Lesson 14)

Key	Answer
You have a car.	*You have a car, don't you?*
He's a nice guy.	*He's a nice guy, isn't he?*
We needed a hard test.	*We needed a hard test, didn't we?*
John won't come to school tomorrow.	*John won't come to school tomorrow, will he?*

1. I'm a nice person.	...
2. We're going to school tomorrow.	...
3. He saw the movie.	...
4. Jason and you are students.	...
5. She is very happy today.	...
6. Next week is Chuseok.	...
7. The cat was playful.	...
8. I'm not mean.	...
9. We didn't see a movie last week.	...
10. My glasses aren't in my bag.	...
11. The professors like us.	...
12. They can study together.	...
13. The stapler is on the desk.	...
14. The computers aren't broken.	...
15. He bought a new smartphone.	...
16. The car needs an oil change.	...
17. Maria doesn't like kimchi.	...
18. We could go to a coffee shop	...
19. The curtains aren't pretty.	...
20. Mass is held on Sunday.	...

Drill #2: Q&A and Free Response

(What do you like? / What are you like?) [a review of Lesson 16]

Key	Answer
What do you like?	*(Free Response) I like apples and oranges.*
What are you like?	*(Free Response) I am a nice and smart person.*
What is your apartment like?	*(Free Response) It is on the 6th floor, and it is small.*

1. What is your family like?	**9. What do your neighbors like?**
2. What does your family like?	**10. What do you like?**
3. What is your neighborhood like?	**11. What are you like?**
4. What are your classmates like?	**12. What does he like?**
5. What do your classmates like?	**13. What is he like?**
6. What does your father like?	**14. What do we all like?**
7. What is your school like?	**15. What are we all like?**
8. What are your neighbors like?	**16. What do dogs like?**

Conversations

Conversation: Community

1. Why do neighbors sometimes argue?
   a) Neighbors often argue because there is too much noise.
   b) I think neighbors argue because they don't know each other very well.

2. What are the benefits of knowing your neighbors?
   a) If I know my neighbors, I will feel much safer in my neighborhood.
   b) Neighbors are usually very friendly, so I can meet them and be friends.

3. Do you ever litter?
   a) Yes, I do. There are not enough trash cans in public places.
   b) No, I don't. I always hold my trash until I find a trash can.

4. Have you ever done any volunteer work?
   a) Yes, I have. I have helped at a local orphanage.
   b) No, I haven't. But, I hope that I can volunteer for community cleanup.

5. Are there good grade schools in your community?
   a) Yes, there are. There are several decent grade schools in my neighborhood.
   b) No, there aren't. My community needs to have better grade schools.

6. Does your community have good parks?
   a) Yes, it does. There are two good parks that are very beautiful and fun.
   b) No, it doesn't. There is only one small park for children to play in.

7. How is health care in your neighborhood?
   a) There is a big hospital in my neighborhood. So, the health care is very good.
   b) I think it is not good because there are few clinics.

8. Are you a member of any online social groups?
   a) Yes, I am. I joined the Nike brand group on Facebook.
   b) Yes, I am. I often play online multiplayer games, such as League of Legends.

9. How active is your community?
   a) My community is very active. People usually go to church, exercise, and shop.
   b) My community is not active. It is a very quiet and peaceful place.

10. Do you want to move to another city?
   a) Yes, I do. I want to live in Seoul because it is more exciting than where I live.
   b) No, I don't. I love this city because it has many opportunities.

11. What does this community need to improve?
    a) This community needs better education systems, such as more learning centers.
    b) I think that this community needs a better police force because crime is too high.

12. Are people nice in your hometown?
    a) Yes, they are. People are always very friendly in my hometown.
    b) No, they aren't. People are not nice there because they are too busy.

13. Were you born and raised in this city?
    a) Yes, I was. My family has lived here since I was born.
    b) No, I wasn't. I moved here when I came to this university.

14. Have you ever helped a stranger?
    a) Yes, I have. I helped a stranger who needed help with a flat tire.
    b) No, I haven't. I am afraid to help a stranger because I don't know the person.

15. Do you have a favorite local sports team?

16. What are some good places to hang out in your city?

17. Does your hometown have a clean environment?

18. Is crime a problem where you live?

19. Is there a lot of English used in your community?

20. Does your community have a unique culture?

Extra Practice:

– Review the previous questions with your group, or ask new questions.

– Try some free talking today.

Lesson 18

Pronunciation

Part Ⅰ : /s/ & /z/

Part Ⅱ : /ts/

Drills

Part Ⅰ : Q&A – "wh-" questions for clarification

Substitution – time expressions

Article – Tips for Success at College

Part Ⅱ : Article – Facebook

Article – KakaoTalk

Conversations

Part Ⅰ : University

Part Ⅱ : Free Discussion (Essay Writing / Final Paper)

Part I

Today's Proverb

"Walk softly, and carry a big stick."

Pronunciation

/s/ & /z/: Seal & Zeal

A review of /s/ and /z/ through minimal pairing.

Beginning	Middle	End
seal - zeal	faces - phases	fleece - fleas
sip - zip	lacy - lazy	peace - peas
sing - zing	doses - dozes	rice - rise
sue - zoo	fussy - fuzzy	loose - lose
C - Z	races - raises	sauce - saws
sack-Zack	racer - razor	basis - bases

1. I saw the lions and tigers loose at the zoo.
2. "C–Z–C–Z–C–Z–C–Z" is easy to say.
3. Someone left their razor on the sink.
4. Rice is one of the basic foods in South Korea.
5. This university has good professors and students!
6. This was an easy class because it was certainly fun.

Drills

Drill #1: Q&A Drill

(who, what, when, where) for clarification

Key	Answer
write a letter this morning ***what***	*I wrote a letter this morning.* *What did you do this morning?*
1. visit my uncle last weekend **2. what**	I visited ... ...did you do last weekend?
3. go to Seoul yesterday **4. where**	I went ... ... did you go yesterday?
5. see my friends just before class **6. who**	I saw ... Who did you see ...?
7. have a sandwich two hours ago **8. when**	...had ... When did ...?
9. have an interview the day before yesterday. **10. what**	I ... What did ... do ...?
11. go fishing in Haeundae **12. where**	... went ... ...did ...?
13. talk to my mother on the phone **14. who**	....did ...talk ...?
15. take a bath this afternoon **16. when**	... ...?
17. apply for jobs all day long **18. what**	... ...?
19. go to a rock concert last Monday **20. where**	... ...?

Drill #2: Substitution Drill

(time expressions)

Key	Answer
Go to a gym-every morning	*I go to a gym every morning.*
Every evening	*I go to a gym every evening.*
Jennifer	*Jennifer goes to a gym every evening.*

1. take a shower	Jennifer takes … every evening.
2. hang out with her friends	Jennifer hangs … every evening.
3. everyday	Jennifer hangs …with her friends everyday.
4. I	…hang out … everyday.
5. memorize English words	I memorize English words ...
6. every Sunday	… every Sunday.
7. go to a temple	… to a temple every Sunday.
8. once a month	I … once a month.
9. play computer games	I play … a month.
10. every weekend	I play … weekend.
11. My brother	…plays … every weekend.
12. every other day	… plays … games every … day.
13. go to movies	My brother … every other day.
14. every month	My brother goes ...
15. go hiking	My brother goes ...
16. every Wednesday	My … every Wednesday.
17. I	I ...
18. get a hair cut	…
19. every two months	…
20. email my high school friends	…

Drill #3: Article

Tips for Success at College

1. **Find Your Perfect Place to Study**: It's important to get your work done, such as your homework, studying for a test, or a project. You need to find the best place for you so that you can maximize your work done and minimize your stress. The best place for you might be the library, a coffee shop, or even an empty classroom. Wherever you go, make it is a place where you can avoid distractions.
2. **Form Good Study Habits**: Many university students notoriously procrastinate on assignments and cram for tests the night before. Make good study habits by studying and doing coursework every day. You can use time between classes or use some of your lunch break to get some extra work done. Good study habits will help you get good grades.
3. **Get Enough Sleep**: Just because your school days are shorter than when you were in grade school, you still need to get enough sleep in order to be able to feel refreshed and motivated to study. Becoming sleepy in class is a sign that you are not getting enough sleep or not focusing on your studies enough. Be extra careful not to doze off in front of your professor! Not only will he be annoyed with you, but you may miss some information.
4. **Form Positive Relationships – Lots of Them**: Do your best to meet new people in school and make new friends. Some of your college relationships will last through most of your life. The friends you make in school can help you in many ways. Clubs are another great way to make friends. Be empathic, and accept differences in others. After all, it's just as William Cowper said in 1785, "Variety is the spice of life."
5. **Talk to Your Professors**: Professors are almost always happy to talk to their students outside of class. Many of them chose a career in teaching because they are happy to meet people and socialize. Don't be afraid to visit your professor's office and talk. Not only can you ask questions, but

you can also get some valuable advice to improve your grades. Professors can sometimes even help you find work after you graduate.

6. **Be Professional**: Remember that school is training you for work in the real world. When you go to class, you need to be a professional. During class, you should pay close attention, take notes, be serious, and do your best. It is often very bad to miss work, so you should also not miss class either. Acting like a professional in class is one way to prepare yourself for being a professional in your future job.
7. **Be Passionate, and Don't Be Discouraged by Failure**: Don't just chase an 'A'. Neil deGrasse Tyson, a famous astrophysicist, stated, "... no one ever asks you what your grades were. Grades become irrelevant. ... ambition and innovation trump grades every time." Even if you fail, remember that failure is a learning experience. Nothing can defeat you if you maintain an optimistic view.
8. **Check Your Test Again**: Watch out for mistakes on your test. Check your test one more time to make sure you didn't write the wrong answer or misunderstand a sentence. Keep an eye on the clock to make sure you have your time organized well to complete each part of the test without rushing. Do the easiest questions first to get them out of the way. On multiple choice answers, try to eliminate wrong answers if you are unsure of the right one.
9. **Contribute**: Don't go quietly into oblivion at your school. Make a name for yourself through positive deeds and a reputation for good contributions. University is a special time in your life that only comes once and is gone. Make great memories and leave your mark that can motivate yourself and others who follow you for years to come.

Conversations

Conversation: University

1. What is your major?
   a) I'm majoring in business administration.
   b) I'm an economics major.

2. What year are you?
   a) I'm a sophomore. This is my 4th semester.
   b) I'm a 3rd year student.

3. Why did you choose your major?
   a) I was always interested in business, so I chose my major.
   b) I want to start my own business later, and I heard the professors were good.

4. What qualities do you need for your major?
   a) I need a good ability to speak in English for my major.
   b) Good presentation skills and mathematic skills are necessary for my major.

5. Do you enjoy studying your major?
   a) Yes, I do. I like my major a lot. It's very interesting.
   b) No, not really. It is a little more difficult than I thought. I'm not good at math.

6. How much time do you spend studying your major?
   a) I study for my major's classes about one hour everyday.
   b) I spend around 3 hours doing homework every week.

7. What is your favorite class?
   a) My favorite class is English Conversation. I really like the English discussion time.
   b) I like marketing most because I'm interested in advertising and consumer behavior.

8. Which professor is the most difficult?
   a) Professor Kim is the most difficult professor. He gives a lot of homework.
   b) Professor Lee is very strict in class, so I think he's the most difficult.

9. How often did you come here during the week this semester?
   a) I came to school 5 days a week.
   b) I came to school on Monday, Tuesday, and Thursday this semester.

10. Are you in any clubs in the university?
   a) I am a member of the Biz Frontier Club. We are learning how to find a good job and write a resume.
   b) I am in the weight lifting club. We go to the gym on campus and lift weights together for encouragement.

11. Do you usually study in the university library?
   a) Yes, I do. I go to the library almost every day.
   b) No, I don't. I prefer to study at home.

12. Who do you usually study with?
   a) I usually study with my classmates. I think two heads are better than one.
   b) I study alone at home because I can't focus on studying in a group.

13. Where do you usually eat lunch?
   a) I usually eat lunch in the cafeteria. The food there is pretty decent.
   b) I like to eat at restaurants in front of the university. Cafeteria food is not very appealing to me.

14. What will you do this vacation?
    a) I will take English class and prepare for a TOEIC test.
    b) I will get a job this vacation because I need some extra money.

15. How often do you hang out with your classmates?
    a) I hang out with them every weekend.
    b) I almost never hang out with them. I'm usually too busy.

16. Will you come to the university this vacation to study?

17. Have you ever taken a semester off from the university?

18. What do you plan to do after graduation?

19. Who do you talk to when you have a problem in your university?

20. What classes did you take this semester?

Part Ⅱ

Today's Idiom

"His bark is worse than his bite."

Pronunciation

/ts/: Sports

It is important when saying /–ts/ as an ending that your /s/ is clearly an 's' sound. /ts/ is used as an ending or middle sound, so remember that the /t/ must be heard as a stop. Practice /sts/ to understand how the /t/ should stop. (eg. lists)

Beginning	Middle	End
-	outside	sports
-	short skirt	shirts
-	artsy	advertisements
-	bitsy	markets
-	bestseller	lists
-	market segment	darts

1. I always wear shirts, pants, and hats when I go outside.
2. Why do girls always wear shorts or mini–skirts in the summer?
3. He plays sports and throws darts at advertisements.
4. Many market scholars study market segments.
5. I saw some lists on websites about the new bestsellers.
6. Artsy advertisements are trendy.

Drills

Drill #1: Article

Facebook

(adapted from: http://en.wikipedia.org/wiki/Facebook)

Vocabulary Words

privately owned, notifications, college, characteristics, fellow students, initially, gradually, ranked, decade, "How on earth...?", to stalk, exes (an ex), to bug our friends, rousing

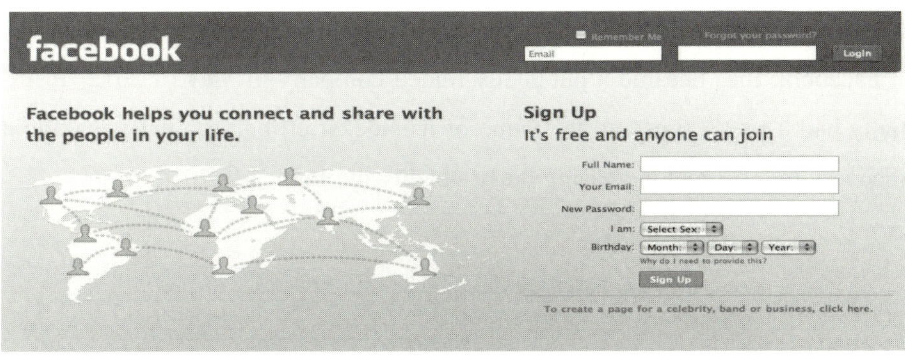

Facebook is a social networking service and website launched in February 2004 and is operated and privately owned by Facebook, Inc. As of January 2014, Facebook has more than 1.23 billion active users with just under a billion mobile users. Users may create a personal profile, add other users as friends, exchange messages, and post status updates. Additionally, users may join common-interest user groups that are organized by workplace, school or college, or other characteristics. The name "Facebook" came from the name for a book given to students at the start of an academic year by university administrations in the United States to help students get to know each other better. Facebook allows any users who are at least 13 years old to become registered users of the website.

Facebook was founded by Mark Zuckerberg with his college roommates and fellow computer science students; Eduardo Saverin, Dustin Moskovitz, and Chris Hughes. The website's membership was initially limited by the founders to Harvard students but was expanded to other colleges in the Boston area, the Ivy League, and Stanford University. It gradually added support for students at various other universities before opening to high school students and finally, to anyone aged 13 and over.

A January 2009 Compete.com study ranked Facebook as the most used social networking service by worldwide monthly active users. Entertainment Weekly included the site on its end-of-the-decade "best-of" list, saying, "How on earth did we stalk our exes, remember our co-workers' birthdays, bug our friends, and play a rousing game of Scrabulous before Facebook?"

Facebook Inc. became a publically traded company in May of 2012. It initially had a rocky start and the value of its stocks fell before finally making a recovery in 2013 and increasing fairly steadily through early 2014.

Comprehension Questions:

1. What is Facebook?
2. How many users are active on Facebook?
3. What can you do on Facebook?
4. Who can become a registered user on Facebook?
5. Who created Facebook?
6. What did Entertainment Weekly say about Facebook?
7. What happened to Facebook's stock values in 2012?

Discussion Questions:

1. Have you ever used Facebook? If so, what do you think of it? If not, why not?
2. Have you ever used Cyworld? If so, what do you think of it? If not, why not?
3. Do you think advertising on social networking sites is effective?
4. Why do people use social networking sites?
5. Do you think social networking sites are a waste of time?
6. How often do you use the Internet? What do you do online?
7. Do you ever visit your friends' homepages, blogs, or Facebook wall?
8. Are you worried about your privacy online?
9. Why do you think Facebook doesn't allow children younger than 13 to make an account?
10. How many hours do you spend on the Internet every week?
11. How many computers does your family have?
12. Do any of your family members use social networking sites?
13. Have you ever used the Internet to track down old friends?
14. What are some other things the Internet is useful for?
15. Do you prefer to watch television programs and movies on TV or on the computer through the Internet?
16. Do you think the Internet is making people lazier? How?

17. Can your cell phone access the Internet? If so, how often do you use the Internet via your cell phone?
18. How do you keep in touch with your friends?
19. What are the consequences of being more connected with friends, co-workers, and family around the world?
20. What are some ways to meet new people on the Internet?
21. How do you protect your computer from viruses and hackers?
22. Have you ever had your online account hacked?

Drill #2: Article

KakaoTalk

(adapted from: http://en.wikipedia.org/wiki/KakaoTalk)

Created in 2006, KakaoTalk is a free application for mobile phones that is available for several operating systems, including Android and iOS. It gives free use of file transfers of videos and photos, text messaging, and phone services. Users can enter into a chat window with a friend or invite several into a group chat.

KakaoTalk adds friends automatically based on the contact list on the user's smartphone. Users can also find friends using KakaoTalk's search feature or through friend recommendations provided by the program.

Since 2011, KakaoTalk has been attempting to expand into a more global market and has used TV commercials in places such as Indonesia, Vietnam, and the Philippines with famous stars from K-pop like Big Bang. While most of the users of the application are in Korea, KakaoTalk has seen a rise in international users, such as in Japan, and hopes to continue this trend into the future.

Comprehension Questions:

1. What is KakaoTalk?
2. How can users add friends to KakaoTalk?
3. What has KakaoTalk been trying to do since 2011?
4. What countries has KakaoTalk been trying to expand in?

Discussion Questions:

1. Do you use KakaoTalk?
2. Do you still send SMS text messages?
3. Why do Koreans prefer to use KakaoTalk instead of other messaging applications?
4. Have you ever used KakaoTalk's video phone call function?
5. How much would you pay to use KakaoTalk if it was no longer free?
6. Is it ok to use KakaoTalk to contact a friend late at night?
7. What other messaging applications do you use?

Conversations

Free Discussion (Essay Writing / Final Paper)

1. Companies and employees use the Internet social media for a variety of reasons. What are some of the benefits that social media, such as Facebook and KakaoTalk, gives to companies and their employees?
2. People attend university for many reasons. What are the reasons that you attend university, or why do you think it is important for students to attend university?
3. Domestic jobs are very important to people of this country, especially to students who are graduating from university soon. Yet, many people prefer to support foreign brands for their major purchases, such as Apple, BMW, and Sony. Why don't people buy domestically more often to support the local job market?
4. In the U.S., teenagers often have part-time jobs while they are still in high school. In South Korea, high school students have very little time to work, and they often do not have any work experience until after they finish college. Do you think it is better for teenagers to work to gain valuable life experiences or to stay in school and study instead? Explain your reasoning.
5. Technology has been changing the way we live our lives for many years. Now, people have access to information through their mobile devices and can easily find information they need whenever necessary. What are the benefits of learning and memorizing information in school if that information can easily be found on a mobile gadget?

Appendix

1. Drill Answers
2. Conversation Tests

1. Drill Answers

Lesson 01

Part I – Drill #2

1. Answer the question.	Please, answer the question.
2. Write the sentence.	Please, write the sentence.
3. Listen carefully.	Please, listen carefully.
4. Repeat after me.	Please, repeat after me.
5. Don't use your dictionary.	Please, don't use your dictionary.
6. Don't answer your cell phone.	Please, don't answer your cell phone.
7. Turn over your paper.	Please, turn over your paper.
8. Raise your hand.	Please, raise your hand.
9. Do number six.	Please, do number six.
10. Stand up.	Please, stand up.
11. Turn in your test.	Please, turn in your test.
12. Work together.	Please, work together.
13. Speak English.	Please, speak English.

* Replace "Please" with "May I", "Could I", or "Can I".

Part Ⅱ – Drill #1

1. reading	I like reading.
2. dancing	I like dancing.
3. watching TV	I like watching TV.
4. singing	I like singing.
5. sleeping	I like sleeping.
6. to read	I like to read.
7. to sing	I like to sing.
8. to watch movies	I like to watch movies.
9. to play sports	I like to play sports.
10. to go to school	I like to go to school.
11. to eat fast food	I like to eat fast food.
12. doing homework	I like doing homework.
13. speaking English	I like speaking English.
14. learning languages	I like learning languages.
15. drinking coffee	I like drinking coffee.

Part Ⅱ – Drill #2

1. engineering	I'm an engineering major.
2. law	I'm a law major.
3. management	I'm a management major.
4. English	I'm an English major.
5. business administration	I'm a business administration major.
6. biology	I'm a biology major.
7. music	I'm a music major.
8. chemistry	I'm a chemistry major.
9. nursing	I'm a nursing major.
10. geology	I'm a geology major.
11. Japanese	I'm a Japanese major.
12. public affairs	I'm a public affairs major.
13. information technology	I'm an information technology major.
14. distribution management	I'm a distribution management major.
15. radiology	I'm a radiology major.

Lesson 02

Part I – Drill #1

1. (question)	Is he a teacher?
2. biologist	Is he a biologist?
3. I	Am I a biologist?
4. you	Are you a biologist?
5. flight attendant	Are you a flight attendant?
6. (statement)	You are a flight attendant.
7. taxi driver	You are a taxi driver.
8. he	He is a taxi driver.
9. we	We are taxi drivers.
10. I	I am a taxi driver.
11. (negative)	I'm not a taxi driver.
12. professor	I'm not a professor.
13. she	She's not a professor.
14. they	They're not professors.
15. you	You're not a professor.
16. (affirmative)	You're a professor
17. lawyer	You're a lawyer.
18. I	I am a lawyer.
19. she	She's a lawyer.
20. we	We're lawyers.

Part I – Drill #2

1. sleepy	Are you sleepy?
2. (negative)	Aren't you sleepy?
3. he	Isn't he sleepy?
4. (statement)	He isn't sleepy.
5. bored	He isn't bored.
6. (affirmative)	He is bored.
7. they	They are bored.
8. I	I am bored.
9. happy	I am happy.
10. we	We are happy.
11. (question)	Are we happy?
12. kind	Are we kind?
13. (negative)	Aren't we kind?
14. you	Aren't you kind?
15. (statement)	You aren't kind.
16. she	She isn't kind.
17. angry	She isn't angry.
18. (affirmative)	She is angry.
19. I	I am angry.
20. they	They are angry.
21. (question)	Are they angry?
22. unkind	Are they unkind?
23. (negative)	Aren't they unkind?
24. he	Isn't he unkind?
25. (statement)	He isn't unkind.
26. she	She isn't unkind.
27. (affirmative)	She is unkind.
28. I	I am unkind.
29. we	We are unkind.
30. you	You are unkind.

Part Ⅱ – Drill #1

1. is	The apple is delicious.
2. sweet	The apple is sweet.
3. (question)	Is the apple sweet?
4. it	Is it sweet?
5. the oranges	Are the oranges sweet?
6. sour	Are the oranges sour?
7. (statement)	The oranges are sour.
8. they	They're sour.
9. it	It's sour.
10. fresh	It's fresh.
11. the vegetables	The vegetables are fresh.
12. (negative)	The vegetables aren't fresh.
13. they	They're not fresh.
14. (affirmative)	They're fresh.
15. salty	They're salty.
16. it	It is salty.
17. (question)	Is it salty?
18. the fish	Is the fish salty?
19. (negative)	Isn't the fish salty?
20. (statement)	The fish isn't salty.
21. the French fries	The French fries aren't salty.
22. (affirmative)	The French fries are salty.
23. they	They are salty.
24. burned	They are burned.
25. the steak	The steak is burned.
26. (negative)	The steak isn't burned.
27. the steaks	The steaks aren't burned.
28. it	It isn't burned.
29. they	They aren't burned.
30. (affirmative)	They are burned.

Lesson 03

Part I – Drill #1

1. How is your father?	He is happy.
2. How is your friend?	She is great.
3. How are the apples?	They are wonderful.
4. How is the weather?	It is rainy.
5. How is this class?	It is difficult.
6. How is your computer?	It is broken.
7. How are your parents?	They are sick.
8. How is the music?	It is loud.
9. How are your friends?	They are nice.
10. How are the pies?	They are sour.
11. How is McDonald's?	It is cheap.
12. How are you all?	We are tired.
13. How is your professor?	He is strict.
14. How is your sister?	She is doing well.
15. How is your brother?	He is studying hard.
16. How is that restaurant?	It is luxurious.
17. How is the coffee?	It is too strong.
18. How are you?	I am optimistic.
19. How is my look?	It is excellent.
20. How is your apartment?	It is just the right size.
21. How are foreigners in Korea?	They are very curious.
22. How is your cold?	It is doing better than last week.
23. How is your English?	It is improving day by day.
24. How are the students?	They are diligent.
25. How is your friend's family?	It is large.
26. How are they?	They are angry.
27. How is the bathroom?	It is very dirty.
28. How is the weather in winter?	It is quite cold.
29. How are the flowers in spring?	They are very lovely.
30. How are you and your family?	We are a little busy these days.

* Answers will vary.

Part I – Drill #2

1. generous	He is a generous man.
2. optimistic	He is an optimistic man.
3. cheerful	He is a cheerful man.
4. easy-going	He is an easy-going man.
5. unkind lady	She is an unkind lady.
6. cold	She is a cold lady.
7. mean	She is a mean lady.
8. pessimistic	She is a pessimistic lady.
9. miserable	She is a miserable lady.
10. man	He is a miserable man.
11. weak	He is a weak man.
12. honest	He is an honest man.
13. clever	He is a clever man.
14. shy	He is a shy man.
15. good-looking	He is a good-looking man.
16. gentle	He is a gentle man.
17. cute	He is a cute man.
18. woman	She is a cute woman.
19. beautiful	She is a beautiful woman.
20. lovely	She is a lovely woman.
21. sensitive	She is a sensitive woman.
22. extroverted	She is an extroverted woman.
23. lazy	She is a lazy woman.
24. introverted	She is an introverted woman.
25. hard-working	She is a hard-working woman.
26. man	He is a hard-working man.
27. reliable	He is a reliable man.
28. flexible	He is a flexible man.
29. good	He is a good man.
30. dishonest	He is a dishonest man.

Lesson 04

Part I – Drill #1

1. Madison, acrobat	Is Madison an acrobat?
2. Aaron, actor	Is Aaron an actor?
3. Emily, anchor woman	Is Emily an anchor woman?
4. Ethan, manager	Is Ethan a manager?
5. (sentence)	Ethan is a manager.
6. Ryan, announcer	Ryan is an announcer.
7. Isabella, editor	Isabella is an editor.
8. Jack, bus driver	Jack is a bus driver.
9. Joshua, movie director	Joshua is a movie director.
10. Chloe, consultant	Chloe is a consultant.
11. Logan, designer	Logan is a designer.
12. (question)	Is Logan a designer?
13. McKenna, counselor	Is McKenna a counselor?
14. Kylie, chef	Is Kylie a chef?
15. Benjamin, clerk	Is Benjamin a clerk?
16. Elijah, cashier	Is Elijah a cashier?
17. (sentence)	Elijah is a cashier.
18. Ian, bartender	Ian is a bartender.
19. Daniel, athlete	Daniel is an athlete.
20. Colin, astronaut	Colin is an astronaut.

Part I – Drill #2

1. selfish	Are you a selfish boy?
2. she	Is she a selfish girl?
3. they	Are they selfish girls?
4. foolish	Are they foolish girls?
5. reckless	Are they reckless girls?
6. (sentence)	They are reckless girls.
7. Jenna	Jenna is a reckless girl.
8. he	He is a reckless boy.
9. smart	He is a smart boy.
10. thoughtless	He is a thoughtless boy.
11. (negative)	He isn't a thoughtless boy.
12. you	You aren't a thoughtless boy.
13. good	You aren't a good boy.
14. (affirmative)	You are a good boy.
15. careful	You are a careful boy.
16. they	They are careful boys.
17. (question)	Are they careful boys?
18. dangerous	Are they dangerous boys?
19. he	Is he a dangerous boy?
20. we	Are we dangerous boys?

Part Ⅱ – Drill #1

1. Sam, kind announcer	Is Sam a kind announcer?
2. Yes	Yes, he's a very kind announcer.
3. No	No, he's not a very kind announcer.
4. Isabella, skillful editor	Is Isabella a skillful editor?
5. Yes	Yes, she's a very skillful editor.
6. No	No, she's not a very skillful editor.
7. Jack, lazy bus driver	Is Jack a lazy bus driver?
8. Yes	Yes, he's a very lazy bus driver.
9. No	No, he's not a very lazy bus driver.
10. Chloe, successful consultant	Is Chloe a successful consultant?
11. Yes	Yes, she's a very successful consultant.
12. No	No, she's not a very successful consultant.
13. Jenny, funny counselor	Is Jenny a funny counselor?
14. Yes	Yes, she's a very funny counselor.
15. No	No, she's not a very funny counselor.
16. Benjamin, quiet clerk	Is Benjamin a quiet clerk?
17. Yes	Yes, he's a very quiet clerk.
18. No	No, he's not a very quiet clerk.
19. Ethan, patient manager	Is Ethan a patient manager?
20. Yes	Yes, he's a very patient manager.
21. No	No, he's not a very patient manager.

Part Ⅱ – Drill #2

1. this supermarket - cheap **2. No - expensive**	Is this supermarket cheap? No, it isn't a cheap supermarket. It's an expensive supermarket.
3. this car - dangerous **4. No - safe**	Is this car dangerous? No, it isn't a dangerous car. It's a safe car.
5. the girl - tall **6. No - short**	Is the girl tall? No, she isn't a tall girl. She's a short girl.
7. this bag - heavy **8. No - light**	Is this bag heavy? No, it isn't a heavy bag. It's a light bag.
9. these - strong windows **10. No - weak**	Are these strong windows? No, they aren't strong windows. They are weak windows.
11. the teacher - strict **12. No - lenient**	Is the teacher strict? No, he isn't a strict teacher. He is a lenient teacher.
13. the kids - good **14. No - bad**	Are the kids good? No, they aren't good kids. They are bad kids.
15. he - mean clerk **16. No - nice**	Is he a mean clerk? No, he isn't a mean clerk. He is a nice clerk.
17. the water - hot **18. No - cold**	Is the water hot? No, it isn't hot water. It's cold water.
19. it - dirty room **20. No - clean**	Is it a dirty room? No, it isn't a dirty room. It's a clean room.

Lesson 05

Part I – Drill #1

1. a comb **2. (affirmative)** **3. (negative)**	Do you want a comb? Thanks, I need a comb. Thanks, but I already have a comb.
4. a handkerchief **5. (affirmative)** **6. (negative)**	Do you want a handkerchief? Thanks, I need a handkerchief. Thanks, but I already have a handkerchief.
7. a hair band **8. (affirmative)** **9. (negative)**	Do you want a hair band? Thanks, I need a hair band. Thanks, but I already have a hair band.
10. a laptop **11. (affirmative)** **12. (negative)**	Do you want a laptop? Thanks, I need a laptop. Thanks, but I already have a laptop.
13. a notebook **14. (affirmative)** **15. (negative)**	Do you want a notebook? Thanks, I need a notebook. Thanks, but I already have a notebook.
16. a battery **17. (affirmative)** **18. (negative)**	Do you want a battery? Thanks, I need a battery. Thanks, but I already have a battery.
19. a pencil lead **20. (affirmative)** **21. (negative)**	Do you want a pencil lead? Thanks, I need a pencil lead. Thanks, but I already have a pencil lead.

Part I – Drill #2

1. a big bag - have	Do you have a big bag? No, I have a small bag.
2. hot tea - want	Do you want hot tea? No, I want cold tea
3. a smart dog - have	Do you have a smart dog? No, I have a stupid dog.
4. spicy sauce - want	Do you want spicy sauce? No, I want mild sauce.
5. a hard bed - have	Do you have a hard bed? No, I have a soft bed.
6. an expensive watch - want	Do you want an expensive watch? No, I want a cheap watch?
7. a dull knife - have	Do you have a dull knife? No, I have a sharp knife.
8. a loud voice - have	Do you have a loud voice? No, I have a quiet voice.
9. a tall girlfriend - want	Do you want a tall girlfriend? No, I want a short girlfriend.
10. curly hair - have	Do you have curly hair? No, I have straight hair.

Part Ⅱ – Drill #1

1. movie directors	What do movie directors do?
2. movies, make	They make movies.
3. pharmacists	What do pharmacists do?
4. medicine, prepare	They prepare medicine.
5. doctors	What do doctors do?
6. patients, examine	They examine patients.
7. architects	What do architects do?
8. buildings, construct	They construct buildings.
9. veterinarians	What do veterinarians do?
10. animals, examine	They examine animals.
11. manufacturers	What do manufacturers do?
12. products, manufacture	They manufacture products.
13. English teachers	What do English teachers do?
14. English, teach	They teach English.
15. managers	What do managers do?
16. affairs, manage	They manage affairs.
17. security guards	What do security guards do?
18. places, guard	They guard places.
19. flight attendants	What do flight attendants do?
20. passengers, serve	They serve passengers.

Lesson 06

Part I – Drill #1

1. go to the gym	Does he ever go to the gym?
2. you	Do you ever go to the gym?
3. listen to the news	Do you ever listen to the news?
4. cook for yourself	Do you ever cook for yourself?
5. wash dishes	Do you ever wash dishes?
6. play the piano	Do you ever play the piano?
7. they	Do they ever play the piano?
8. ride bicycles	Do they ever ride bicycles?
9. read English newspapers	Do they ever read English newspapers?
10. buy and sell stocks	Do they ever buy and sell stocks?
11. you	Do you ever buy and sell stocks?
12. he	Does he ever buy and sell stocks?
13. go out to eat	Does he ever go out to eat?
14. go fishing	Does he ever go fishing?
15. watch CNN	Does he ever watch CNN?
16. go camping	Does he ever go camping?
17. she	Does she ever go camping?
18. they	Do they ever go camping?
19. call their friends	Do they ever call their friends?
20. write letters	Do they ever write letters?

Part I – Drill #2

1. usually	I'm usually nervous.
2. watch CNN	I usually watch CNN.
3. often	I often watch CNN.
4. he	He often watches CNN.
5. practice English pronunciation	He often practices English pronunciation.
6. never	He never practices English pronunciation.
7. they	They never practice English pronunciation.
8. sometimes	They sometimes practice English pronunciation.
9. play baseball	They sometimes play baseball.
10. always	They always play baseball.
11. rarely	They rarely play baseball.
12. tired	They are rarely tired.
13. she	She is rarely tired.
14. do yoga	She rarely does yoga.
15. seldom	She seldom does yoga.
16. hardly ever	She hardly ever does yoga.
17. I	I hardly ever do yoga.
18. cheerful	I am hardly ever cheerful.
19. often	I am often cheerful.
20. usually	I am usually cheerful.

Part Ⅱ – Drill #1

1. you - tired **always**	Are you ever tired? Yes, I'm always tired.
2. Susan - wear contact lenses **often**	Does Susan ever wear contact lenses? Yes, she often wears contact lenses.
3. you - lonely **often**	Are you ever lonely? Yes, I'm often lonely.
4. Tom - clean his room **always**	Does Tom ever clean his room? Yes, he always cleans his room.
5. you - nervous **always**	Are you ever nervous? Yes, I'm always nervous.
6. Kelly - call her friends **often**	Does Kelly ever call her friends? Yes, she often calls her friends.
7. Lori - happy **often**	Is Lori ever happy? Yes, she's often happy.
8. you - go skating **always**	Do you ever go skating? Yes, I always go skating.
9. Jennifer - angry **often**	Is Jennifer ever angry? Yes, she's often angry.
10. you - play the piano **always**	Do you ever play the piano? Yes, I always play the piano.

Lesson 07

Part I – Drill #1

1. he	Does he have his pens with him?
2. headphones	Does he have his headphones with him?
3. (statement)	He has his headphones with him.
4. you	You have your headphones with you.
5. (negative)	You don't have your headphones with you.
6. Jenny	Jenny doesn't have her headphones with her.
7. (affirmative)	Jenny has her headphones with her.
8. they	They have their headphones with them.
9. money	They have their money with them.
10. I	I have my money with me.
11. (question)	Do I have my money with me?
12. she	Does she have her money with her?
13. (statement)	She has her money with her.
14. Mike and I	Mike and I have our money with us.
15. the kids	The kids have their money with them.
16. (negative)	The kids don't have their money with them.
17. their cat	The kids don't have their cat with them.
18. Jennifer	Jennifer doesn't have her cat with her.
19. he	He doesn't have his cat with him.
20. (affirmative)	He has his cat with him.

Part Ⅱ – Drill #1

1. use - your brush	Can I use your brush? I don't have my brush with me.
2. where - her running shoes	Where are her running shoes? She doesn't have her running shoes with her.
3. use - his umbrella	Can I use his umbrella? He doesn't have his umbrella with him.
4. where - your cell phone	Where is your cell phone? I don't have my cell phone with me.
5. use - their backpack	Can I use their backpack? They don't have their backpack with them.
6. where - our MP3 player	Where is our MP3 player? We don't have our MP3 player with us.
7. use - your jacket	Can I use your jacket? I don't have my jacket with me.
8. where - her scarf	Where is her scarf? She doesn't have her scarf with her.
9. use - their camera	Can I use their camera? They don't have their camera with them.
10. where – his laptop	Where is his laptop? He doesn't have his laptop with him.

Lesson 08

Part I – Drill #1

1. he	He's majoring in English.
2. architecture	He's majoring in architecture.
3. they	They're majoring in architecture.
4. you	You're majoring in architecture.
5. economics	You're majoring in economics.
6. I	I'm majoring in economics.
7. she	She's majoring in economics.
8. music	She's majoring in music.
9. engineering	She's majoring in engineering.
10. education	She's majoring in education.
11. they	They're majoring in education.
12. Chinese	They're majoring in Chinese.
13. philosophy	They're majoring in philosophy.
14. I	I'm majoring in philosophy.
15. physics	I'm majoring in physics.
16. trade	I'm majoring in trade.
17. she	She's majoring in trade.
18. archaeology	She's majoring in archaeology.
19. he	He's majoring in archaeology.
20. accounting	He's majoring in accounting.

Part I – Drill #2

1. where, a computer	Where can you buy a computer?
2. a computer store	You can buy one in a computer store.
3. where, a scarf	Where can you buy a scarf?
4. a clothing store	You can buy one in a clothing store.
5. where, earrings	Where can you buy earrings?
6. a jewelry store	You can buy some in a jewelry store.
7. where, snacks	Where can you buy snacks?
8. a grocery store	You can buy some in a grocery store.
9. where, ice cream	Where can you buy ice cream?
10. an ice cream parlor	You can buy some in an ice cream parlor.
11. where, lotion	Where can you buy lotion?
12. a cosmetics store	You can buy some in a cosmetic store.
13. where, CDs	Where can you buy CDs?
14. a music store	You can buy some in a music store.
15. where, books	Where can you buy books?
16. a bookstore	You can buy some in a bookstore.
17. where, MP3s	Where can you buy MP3s?
18. online	You can buy some online.
19. where, a bicycle	Where can you buy a bicycle?
20. a bike shop	You can buy one in a bike shop.

Part II – Drill #1

1. buy an expensive watch **2.**	Did you buy an expensive watch? No, it was a cheap watch.
3. turn on a bright light **4.**	Did you turn on a bright light? No, it was a dim light
5. use a sharp pencil **6.**	Did you use a sharp pencil? No, it was a dull pencil.
7. wear long socks **8.**	Did you wear long socks No, they were short socks.
9. drink cold tea **10.**	Did you drink cold tea? No, it was hot tea.
11. take a difficult class **12.**	Did you take a difficult class? No, it was an easy class.
13. bring a thick book **14.**	Did you bring a thick book? No, it was a thin book.
15. sit on a clean chair **16.**	Did you sit on a clean chair? No, it was a dirty chair.
17. wear a wet sweater **18.**	Did you wear a wet sweater? No, it was a dry sweater.
19. watch a fun movie **20.**	Did you watch a fun movie? No, it was a boring movie.

Part Ⅱ – Drill #2

1. the kids	The kids were annoyed.
2. confused	The kids were confused.
3. (negative)	The kids weren't confused.
4. he	He wasn't confused.
5. worried	He wasn't worried.
6. you	You weren't worried.
7. (affirmative)	You were worried.
8. fascinated	You were fascinated.
9. she	She was fascinated.
10. I	I was fascinated.
11. (question)	Was I fascinated?
12. invited	Was I invited?
13. they	Were they invited?
14. (statement)	They were invited.
15. relaxed	They were relaxed.
16. Mike	Mike was relaxed.
17. excited	Mike was excited.
18. we	We were excited.
19. interested	We were interested.
20. he	He was interested.

Lesson 09

Part I – Drill #1

1. the room - clean **2.**	Was the room clean? No, it was dirty.
3. the vegetables - fresh **4.**	Were the vegetables fresh? No, they were rotten.
5. the music - loud **6.**	Was the music loud? No, it was quiet.
7. the models - tall **8.**	Were the models tall? No, they were short.
9. the mid-term test - easy **10.**	Was the mid-term test easy? No, it was difficult.
11. the plans - practical **12.**	Were the plans practical? No, they were impractical.
13. the answer - clear **14.**	Was the answer clear? No, it was confusing.
15. the oranges - sweet **16.**	Were the oranges sweet? No, they were sour.
17. the teacher - easygoing **18.**	Was the teacher easygoing? No, he was strict.
19. the athletes - out of shape **20.**	Were the athletes out of shape? No, they were in shape.

Part I – Drill #2

1. have - an eraser **2. yes**	Did you have an eraser? Yes, I had one.
3. wear - the scarf **4. no**	Did you wear the scarf? No, I didn't wear it.
5. take - a test **6. yes**	Did you take a test? Yes, I took one.
7. write - the card **8. no**	Did you write the card? No, I didn't write it.
9. eat - an ice cream cone **10. yes**	Did you eat an ice cream cone? Yes, I ate one.
11. use - the lotion **12. no**	Did you use the lotion? No, I didn't use it.
13. take - a bath **14. no**	Did you take a bath? No, I didn't take one.
15. drink - the milk **16. yes**	Did you drink the milk? Yes, I drank it.
17. take - a walk **18. no**	Did you take a walk? No, I didn't take one.
19. wash - the cup **20. yes**	Did you wash the cup? Yes, I washed it.

Part II – Drill #1

1. sell - hair pins **2. yes**	Did you sell hair pins? Yes, I sold some.
3. light - the candles **4. no**	Did you light the candles? No, I didn't light them.
5. spend - money **6. yes**	Did you spend money? Yes, I spent some.
7. wear - the earrings **8. no**	Did you wear the earrings? No, I didn't wear them.
9. drink - tea **10. no**	Did you drink tea? No, I didn't drink any.
11. take - the classes **12. yes**	Did you take the classes? Yes, I took them.
13. bring - clothes **14. yes**	Did you bring clothes? Yes, I brought some.
15. use - the credit cards **16. yes**	Did you use the credit cards? Yes, I used them.
17. take - transportation **18. no**	Did you take transportation? No, I didn't take any.
19. watch - the movies **20. yes**	Did you watch the movies? Yes, I watched them.

Part Ⅱ – Drill #2

1. She - clean her room **2. last night**	She is cleaning her room. She cleaned her room last night.
3. They - read a newspaper **4. this morning**	They are reading a newspaper. They read a newspaper this morning.
5. I - play the violin **6. yesterday**	I am playing the violin. I played the violin yesterday.
7. He - take a shower **8. last night**	He is taking a shower. He took a shower last night.
9. She - listen to the radio **10. a little while ago**	She is listening to the radio. She listened to the radio a little while ago.
11. We - take a midterm test **12. the day before yesterday**	We are taking a midterm test. We took a midterm test the day before yesterday.
13. They - wear nice shoes **14. this morning**	They are wearing nice shoes. They wore nice shoes this morning.
15. You - go to the beach **16. last summer**	You are going to the beach. You went to the beach last summer.
17. I - wash the dishes **18. about 10 minutes ago**	I am washing the dishes. I washed the dishes about 10 minutes ago.
19. She - watch the soccer game **20. last night**	She is watching the soccer game. She watched the soccer game last night.

Lesson 10

Part Ⅱ – Drill #2

1. We	We went to the park last week.
2. They	They went to the park last week.
3. an hour ago	They went to the park an hour ago.
4. run	They ran an hour ago.
5. swim	They swam an hour ago.
6. last month	They swam last month.
7. go to Seoul	They went to Seoul last month.
8. last winter	They went to Seoul last winter.
9. He	He went to Seoul last winter.
10. study	He studied last winter.
11. dance	He danced last winter.
12. I	I danced last winter.
13. sing	I sang last winter.
14. just before class	I sang just before class.
15. see - the professor	I saw the professor just before class.
16. talk - to my friend	I talked to my friend just before class.
17. on Wednesday	I talked to my friend on Wednesday.
18. watch TV	I watched T.V. on Wednesday.
19. see a good movie	I saw a good movie on Wednesday.
20. take a test	I took a test on Wednesday.
21. read a book	I read a book on Wednesday.
22. last weekend	I read a book last weekend.
23. We	We read a book last weekend.
24. drop by your house	We dropped by your house last weekend.

Lesson 11

Part I – Drill #1

1. car	What kind of car do you want? --- I want a fast one.
2. computer	What kind of computer do you want? --- I want a good one.
3. pens	What kinds of pens do you want? --- I want black ones.
4. bag	What kind of bag do you want? --- I want a big one.
5. friends	What kinds of friends do you want? --- I want outgoing ones.
6. professor	What kind of professor do you want? --- I want a lenient one.
7. camera	What kind of camera do you want? --- I want an expensive one.
8. shirt	What kind of shirt do you want? --- I want a warm one.
9. pants	What kinds of pants do you want? --- I want baggy ones.
10. pillows	What kinds of pillows do you want? --- I want soft ones.
11. house	What kind of house do you want? --- I want a large one.
12. job	What kind of job do you want? --- I want a well-paying one.
13. homework assignments	What kinds of homework assignments do you want? --- I want easy ones.
14. bicycle	What kind of bicycle do you want? --- I want a durable one.
15. hats	What kinds of hats do you want? --- I want fashionable ones.

Part I – Drill #2

1. sleepy	Is he sleepy now?
2. (negative)	Isn't he sleepy now?
3. angry	Isn't he angry now?
4. studying	Isn't he studying now?
5. next week	Won't he be studying next week?
6. (affirmative)	Will he be studying next week?
7. (statement)	He will be studying next week.
8. you	You will be studying next week.
9. taking a test	You will be taking a test next week.
10. yesterday	You were taking a test yesterday.
11. today	You are taking a test today.
12. I	I am taking a test today.
13. sleepy	I am sleepy today.
14. (negative)	I'm not sleepy today.
15. he	He's not sleepy today.
16. (question)	Isn't he sleepy today?
17. tonight	Won't he be sleepy tonight?
18. she	Won't she be sleepy tonight?
19. angry	Won't she be angry tonight?
20. (affirmative)	Will she be angry tonight?
21. going home	Will she be going home tonight?
22. dancing	Will she be dancing tonight?
23. I	Will I be dancing tonight?
24. (statement)	I will be dancing tonight.

Part Ⅱ – Drill #1

1. Is there a car in the garage?	Yes, there is.
2. Is it raining?	No, it isn't.
3. Are you going to school?	Yes, I am.
4. Do you like kimchi?	Yes, I do.
5. Don't you like kimchi?	Yes, I do.
6. Were you at school yesterday?	No, I wasn't.
7. Am I a student?	Yes, you are.
8. Is his name "John"?	No, it isn't.
9. Is your book thick?	Yes, it is.
10. Are you parents tired?	Yes, they are.
11. Isn't there a pencil on the desk?	No, there isn't.
12. Are they good students?	No, they aren't.
13. Is she a nice girl?	No, she isn't.
14. Will you help me?	Yes, I will.
15. Do you like his hat?	No, I don't.
16. Are you cold?	No, I'm not.
17. Is Korea a great country?	Yes, it is.
18. Are there any students in this class?	Yes, there are.
19. Is there a bathroom on this floor?	Yes, there is.
20. Do you have a headache?	No, I don't.
21. Can I borrow your pencil?	No, you can't.
22. Is our university large?	No, it isn't.

∗ Answers may vary.

Part Ⅱ – Drill #2

1. this class - long	Is this class long? No, it isn't. It's short.
2. that cat - old	Is that cat old? No, it isn't. It's young.
3. this cherry - bitter	Is this cherry bitter? No, it isn't. It's sweet.
4. his water bottle - full	Is his water bottle full? No, it isn't. It's empty.
5. that train - fast	Is that train fast? No, it isn't. It's slow
6. this shirt - dirty	Is this shirt dirty? No, it isn't. It's clean.
7. John - married	Is John married? No, he isn't. He's single.
8. this library - public	Is this library public? No, it isn't. It's private.
9. the test - easy	Is the test easy? No, it isn't. It's difficult.
10. the bag - heavy	Is the bag heavy? No, it isn't. It's light.
11. this dog - noisy	Is this dog noisy? No, it isn't. It's quiet.
12. the actor - popular	Is the actor popular? No, he isn't. He is unpopular.
13. this cat - sick	Is this cat sick? No, it isn't. It's healthy.
14. the country - dangerous	Is the country dangerous? No, it isn't. It is safe.
15. this food - spicy	Is this food spicy? No, it isn't. It is mild.

Lesson 12

Part I – Drill #1

1. tomorrow	It will be cheap tomorrow.
2. cheaper	It will be cheaper tomorrow.
3. next week	It will be cheaper next week.
4. on sale	It will be on sale next week.
5. discounted	It will be discounted next week.
6. promoted	It will be promoted next week.
7. the day before yesterday	It was promoted the day before yesterday.
8. last month	It was promoted last month.
9. sold out	It was sold out last month.
10. in stock	It was in stock last month.
11. right now	It is in stock right now.
12. out of stock	It is out of stock right now.
13. full price	It is full price right now.
14. last weekend	It was full price last weekend.
15. next Monday	It will be full price next Monday.
16. half-price	It will be half-price next Monday.
17. 50% off	It will be 50% off next Monday.
18. more expensive	It will be more expensive next Monday.
19. 30% off	It will be 30% off next Monday.
20. a steal	It will be a steal next Monday.
21. in December	It is a steal in December.
22. 15% off	It is 15% off in December.
23. in July	It is 15% off in July.
24. on display	It is on display in July.
25. advertised	It is advertised in July.
26. offered	It is offered in July.
27. sold	It is sold in July.
28. given away	It is given away in July.
29. next December	It will be given away next December.
30. on the weekend	It will be given away on the weekend.

Part I – Drill #2

1. generous	He is a generous boss.
2. optimistic	He is an optimistic boss.
3. supervisor	He is an optimistic supervisor.
4. easy-going	He is an easy-going supervisor.
5. employee	He is an easy-going employee.
6. hard-working	He is a hard-working employee.
7. diligent	He is a diligent employee.
8. employer	He is a diligent employer.
9. suspicious	He is a suspicious employer.
10. thrifty	He is a thrifty employer.
11. customer	He is a thrifty customer.
12. honest	He is an honest customer.
13. clever	He is a clever customer.
14. She	She is a clever customer.
15. concerned	She is a concerned customer.
16. angry	She is an angry customer.
17. satisfied	She is a satisfied customer.
18. They	They are satisfied customers.
19. consumer	They are satisfied consumers.
20. I	I am a satisfied consumer.
21. manager	I am a satisfied manager.
22. extroverted	I am an extroverted manager.
23. lazy	I am a lazy manager.
24. introverted	I am an introverted manager.
25. thoughtful	I am a thoughtful manager.
26. She	She is a thoughtful manager.
27. reliable	She is a reliable manager.
28. flexible	She is a flexible manager.
29. good	She is a good manager.
30. careful	She is a careful manager.

Part Ⅱ – Drill #1

1. that book **2. --- 35,000 won**	How much was that book? --- It cost 35,000 won.
3. those pants **4. --- 65,000 won**	How much were those pants? --- They cost 65,000 won.
5. this cell phone **6. --- 100,000 won**	How much was this cell phone? --- It cost 100,000 won.
7. your pencil **8. --- 500 won**	How much was your pencil? --- It cost 500 won.
9. your electronic dictionary **10. --- 70,000 won**	How much was your electronic dictionary? --- It cost 70,000 won.
11. your mp3 player **12. --- 50,000 won**	How much was your mp3 player? --- It cost 50,000 won.
13. her jacket **14. --- about 150,000 won**	How much was her jacket? --- It cost about 150,000 won.
15. his hat **16. --- 20,000 won**	How much was his hat? --- It cost 20,000 won.
17. that old car **18. --- 5,000,000 won**	How much was that old car? --- It cost 5,000,000 won.
19. your new computer **20. --- 1,000,000 won**	How much was your new computer? --- It cost 1,000,000 won.
21. this bicycle **22. --- 300,000 won**	How much was this bicycle? --- It cost 300,000 won.
23. that lipstick **24. --- 13,000 won**	How much was that lipstick? --- It cost 13,000 won.
25. that bag **26. --- 10,000 won**	How much was that bag? --- It cost 10,000 won.
27. your glasses **28. --- 120,000 won**	How much were your glasses? --- They cost 120,000 won.
29. your notebooks **30. --- 1,800 won**	How much were your notebooks? --- They cost 1,800 won.

Part Ⅱ – Drill #2

1. --- **pencils - 5,000 won**	What did you buy? I bought pencils for 5,000 won.
2. --- **a computer - 1,500,000 won**	What did you buy? I bought a computer for 1,500,000 won.
3. --- **a jump rope - 10,000 won**	What did you buy? I bought a jump rope for 10,000 won.
4. --- **a cup - 1,000 won won**	What did you buy? I bought a cup for 1,000 won.
5. --- **a printer - 45,000 won**	What did you buy? I bought a printer for 45,000 won.
6. --- **a new watch - 80,000 won**	What did you buy? I bought a new watch for 80,000 won.
7. --- **computer paper - 5,000 won**	What did you buy? I bought computer paper for 5,000 won.
8. --- **a new TV - 900,000 won**	What did you buy? I bought a new TV for 900,000 won.
9. --- **some kimchi - 3,000 won**	What did you buy? I bought some kimchi for 3,000 won.
10. --- **eye shadow - 9,000 won**	What did you buy? I bought eye shadow for 9,000 won.
11. --- **a bottle of Pepsi - 1,000 won**	What did you buy? I bought a bottle of Pepsi for 1,000 won.
12. --- **a cheese pizza - 5,000 won**	What did you buy? I bought a cheese pizza for 5,000 won.
13. --- **a pencil case - 1,500 won**	What did you buy? I bought a pencil case for 1,500 won.
14. --- **Nike shoes - 150,000 won**	What did you buy? I bought Nike shoes for 150,000 won.
15. --- **a Basic House shirt - 20,000**	What did you buy? I bought a Basic House shirt for 20,000 won.

Lesson 13

Part Ⅱ – Drill #1

1. his computer	This is his computer.
2. her car	This is her car.
3. mine	This car is mine.
4. yours	This car is yours.
5. our	This is our car.
6. my job	This is my job.
7. theirs	This job is theirs.
8. hers	This job is hers.
9. her	This is her job.
10. is his.	This job is his.
11. ours	This job is ours.
12. their desk	This is their desk.
13. theirs	This desk is theirs.
14. yours	This desk is yours.
15. your	This is your desk.
16. mine	This desk is mine.
17. hers	This desk is hers.
18. our	This is our desk.
19. her	This is her desk.
20. his	This is his desk.

Part Ⅱ – Drill #2

1. this supermarke - cheap **2. ---**	Is this supermarket cheap? No, It isn't a cheap supermarket. It's an expensive supermarket.
3. this gas range - dangerous **4. ---**	Is this gas range dangerous? No, It isn't a dangerous gas range. It's a safe gas range.
5. the girl - tall **6. ---**	Is the girl tall? No, she isn't a tall girl. She's a short girl.
7. this bag - heavy **8. ---**	Is this bag heavy? No, it isn't a heavy bag. It's a light bag.
9. these - strong windows **10. ---**	Are these strong windows? No, they aren't strong windows. They're weak windows.
11. the teacher - strict **12. ---**	Is the teacher strict? No, he isn't a strict teacher. He's a lenient teacher.
13. the kids - good **14. ---**	Are the kids good? No, they aren't good kids. They are bad kids.
15. he - mean clerk **16. ---**	Is he a mean clerk? No, he isn't a mean clerk. He's a nice clerk.
17. the water - hot **18. ---**	Is the water hot? No, it isn't hot water. It's cold water.
19. it - dirty room **20. ---**	Is it a dirty room? No, it isn't a dirty room. It is a clean room.

Lesson 14

Part Ⅱ – Drill #1

1. I went to school because I wanted to learn something.	A: Why did you go to school? B: Because I wanted to learn something.
2. I needed to buy some food because I was hungry.	A: Why did you need to buy some food? B: Because I was hungry.
3. I didn't call my mother because I knew she wasn't home.	A: Why didn't you call your mother? B: Because I knew she wasn't home.
4. I didn't pay the bill because I don't have my wallet.	A: Why didn't you pay the bill? B: Because I don't have my wallet.
5. I helped her today because her job is difficult.	A: Why did you help her today? B: Because her job is difficult.
6. I felt sleepy today because I didn't sleep last night.	A: Why did you feel sleepy today? B: Because I didn't sleep last night.
7. I didn't drive my car because I don't have any gas.	A: Why didn't you drive your car? B: Because I don't have any gas.
8. I didn't check my email because my computer is broken.	A: Why didn't you check your email? B: Because my computer is broken.
9. I finished my homework because I had some free time.	A: Why did you finish your homework? B: Because I had some free time.
10. I brought my umbrella because it's going to rain.	A: Why did you bring your umbrella? B: Because it's going to rain.

Part Ⅱ – Drill #2

1. take, trip	Have you ever taken a trip?
2. see, movie	Have you ever seen a movie?
3. spoke, French	Have you ever spoken French?
4. fight, with, friend	Have you ever fought with a friend?
5. go, abroad	Have you ever gone abroad?
6. meet, famous person	Have you ever met a famous person?
7. be, successful	Have you ever been successful?
8. wear, contacts	Have you ever worn contacts?
9. sing, rock and roll songs	Have you ever sung rock and roll songs?
10. make, kimchi	Have you ever made kimchi?

Lesson 15

Part I – Drill #1

1. I called off the game.	I called it off.
2. He took over the team.	He took it over.
3. I looked over his essay.	I looked it over.
4. The robber gave up the gun.	The robber gave it up.
5. Jerry took off his jacket.	Jerry took it off.
6. Mina put on her makeup.	Mina put it on.
7. We gave back the library books.	We gave them back.
8. They sorted out the problems.	They sorted them out.
9. Wanda put away her pencil.	Wanda put it away.
10. Henry read up on Korean history.	Henry read up on it.
11. Lisa got through with her work.	Lisa got through with it.
12. Jason cleaned up the spill.	Jason cleaned it up.
13. Sarah and I tossed around the ball.	Sarah and I tossed it around.
14. Julie and Liz cheered up their sad friend.	Julie and Liz cheered her up.
15. The tornado blew over the sign.	The tornado blew it over.

Part I – Drill #2

1. Did he call off the game?	Yes, he called it off.
2. Did the professor look over your essay?	Yes, he looked it over.
3. Did Jane toss around the baseball?	Yes, she tossed it around.
4. Did the typhoon blow over the sign?	Yes, it blew it over.
5. Did they clean up the spill?	Yes, they cleaned it up.
6. Did they turn in their homework?	Yes, they turned it in.
7. Did they sort out the problem?	Yes, they sorted it out.
8. Did she read up on Korean history?	Yes, she read up on it.
9. Did you catch up to Sally yesterday?	Yes, I caught up to her.
10. Did the robber give up the gun?	Yes, he gave it up.

Part Ⅱ – Drill #2

1. Who, did, come, school, with	Who did you come to school with?
2. Why, study, English	Why do you study English?
3. What, favorite, food	What is your favorite food?
4. Where, do, do, your, homework	Where do you do your homework?
5. Why, did, skip, lunch	Why did you skip lunch?
6. What, this	What is this?
7. When, call, your, mother	When do you call your mother?
8. Who, best, friend	Who is your best friend?
9. What, favorite, color	What is your favorite color?
10. Where, going, after, class	Where are you going after class?
11. When, you, happy	When are you happy?
12. Why, did, wear, coat	Why did you wear a coat?
13. Where, do, keep, your, books	Where do you keep your books?
14. Who, did, eat, breakfast, with	Who did you eat breakfast with?
15. Why, did, go, bed, late, last night	Why did you go to bed late last night?

Lesson 17

Part I – Drill #1

1. have - an apple **2. yes**	Did you have an apple? Yes, I had one.
3. use - my computer **4. no**	Did you use my computer? No, I didn't use it.
5. take - her book **6. yes**	Did you take her book? Yes, I took it.
7. see - the movie **8. no**	Did you see the movie? No, I didn't see it.
9. sell - a car **10. yes**	Did you sell a car? Yes, I sold one.
11. use - the money **12. no**	Did you use the money? No, I didn't use it.
13. take - a shower **14. no**	Did you take a shower? No, I didn't take one.
15. fix - the pipe **16. yes**	Did you fix the pipe? Yes, I fixed it.
17. take - a picture **18. no**	Did you take a picture? No, I didn't take one.
19. watch - the game **20. yes**	Did you watch the game? Yes, I watched it.

Part I – Drill #2

1. sell - cars **2. yes**	Did you sell any cars? Yes, I sold some.
3. light - candles **4. no**	Did you light the candles? No, I didn't light any.
5. spend - money **6. yes**	Did you spend money? Yes, I spent some.
7. wear - your shoes **8. no**	Did you wear your shoes? No, I didn't wear them.
9. have - tea **10. no**	Did you have tea? No, I didn't have any.
11. hug - your friends **12. yes**	Did you hug your friends? Yes, I hugged them.
13. bring - some clothes **14. yes**	Did you bring some clothes? Yes, I brought some.
15. taste - the peaches **16. yes**	Did you taste the peaches? Yes, I used them.
17. forget - your glasses **18. no**	Did you forget your glasses? No, I didn't forget them.
19. watch - movies **20. yes**	Did you watch movies? Yes, I watched some.

Part Ⅱ – Drill #1

1. I'm a nice person.	..., aren't I?
2. We're going to school tomorrow.	..., aren't we?
3. He saw the movie.	..., didn't he?
4. Jason and you are students.	..., aren't you?
5. She is very happy today.	..., isn't she?
6. Next week is Chuseok.	..., isn't it?
7. The cat was playful.	..., wasn't it?
8. I'm not mean.	..., am I?
9. We didn't see a movie last week.	..., did we?
10. My glasses aren't in my bag.	..., are they?
11. The professors like us.	..., don't they?
12. They can study together.	..., can't they?
13. The stapler is on the desk.	..., isn't it?
14. The computers aren't broken.	..., are they?
15. He bought a new smartphone.	..., didn't he?
16. The car needs an oil change.	..., doesn't it?
17. Maria doesn't like kimchi.	..., does she?
18. We could go to a coffee shop	..., couldn't we?
19. The curtains aren't pretty.	..., are they?
20. Mass is held on Sunday.	..., isn't it?

Lesson 18

Part I – Drill #1

1. visit my uncle last weekend **2. what**	I visited my uncle last weekend. What did you do last weekend?
3. go to Seoul yesterday **4. where**	I went to Seoul yesterday. Where did you go yesterday?
5. see my friends just before class **6. who**	I saw my friends just before class. Who did you see just before class?
7. have a sandwich two hours ago **8. when**	I had a sandwich two hours ago. When did you have a sandwich?
9. have an interview the day before yesterday **10. what**	I had an interview the day before yesterday. What did you do the day before yesterday?
11. go fishing in Haeundae **12. where**	I went fishing in Haeundae. Where did you go fishing?
13. talk to my mother on the phone **14. who**	I talked to my mother on the phone. Who did you talk to on the phone?
15. take a bath this afternoon **16. when**	I took a bath this afternoon. When did you take a bath?
17. apply for jobs all day long **18. what**	I applied for jobs all day long. What did you do all day long?
19. go to a rock concert last Monday **20. where**	I went to a rock concert last Monday. Where did you go last Monday?

Part I – Drill #2

1. take a shower	Jennifer takes a shower every evening.
2. hang out with her friends	Jennifer hangs out with her friends every evening.
3. everyday	Jennifer hangs out with her friends everyday
4. I	I hang out with my friends everyday.
5. memorize English words	I memorize English words everyday.
6. every Sunday	I memorize English words every Sunday.
7. go to a temple	I go to a temple every Sunday.
8. once a month	I go to a temple once a month.
9. play computer games	I play computer games once a month.
10. every weekend	I play computer games every weekend.
11. My brother	My brother plays computer games every weekend.
12. every other day	My brother plays computer games every other day.
13. go to movies	My brother goes to movies every other day.
14. every month	My brother goes to movies every month.
15. go hiking	My brother goes hiking every month.
16. every Wednesday	My brother goes hiking every Wednesday.
17. I	I go hiking every Wednesday.
18. get a hair cut	I get a hair cut every Wednesday.
19. every two months	I get a hair cut every two months.
20. email my high school friends	I email my high school friends every two months.

2. Conversation Tests

Lesson 01

Part I – Conversation: Introduction

1. good afternoon, how, today
2. what, name
3. what, university, attend
4. how, many, there, family
5. what, hobbies
6. why, take, class
7. where, live
8. how, old, you
9. what, favorite, restaurant
10. what, favorite, kind, music
11. where, from
12. how, come, here, today
13. what, favorite kind, Korean food
14. today, happy
15. like, play sports
16. how many, children, want
17. what, major
18. (statement) tell, best friend
19. can, tell, how, get, subway station, here
20. what, usually, do, weekends

Part II – Conversation: Extended Introduction

1. do, want, get, score, good, this class
2. what, do, yesterday afternoon
3. what, do, tomorrow morning
4. do, have, friends, this class
5. what, do, weekends
6. where, lunch, eat, today
7. how, English, study
8. where, buy, those shoes
9. like, Internet, surf
10. like, new people, meeting
11. like, going, beach
12. what kinds, products, like, buy
13. where, favorite, Korean restaurant
14. who, favorite, actor/actress
15. what, want, talk about, this class
16. who, favorite, professor
17. where, usually, study
18. what, favorite, snack
19. (statement) tell, your family
20. what, country, like, travel to

Lesson 02

Part I – Conversation: General Questions

1. who, favorite, movie star
2. who, best friend
3. who, famous soccer player, Korea
4. where, live
5. where, library
6. where, want, Korea, live
7. where, big department store, this city
8. where, study, usually
9. where, yesterday, go
10. what, do, tomorrow
11. what, favorite, ice cream
12. what, lunch, today, eat
13. what, dinner, tonight, eat
14. what time, get up
15. what time, to bed, go, usually
16. when, today, go, home
17. where, after class, go
18. when, see, again, best friend
19. when, cell phone, off, turn
20. when, travel, want

Part II – Conversation: Shopping

1. like, go shopping
2. where, usually, go to buy, clothes
3. like, online shopping
4. which site, usually use, online shopping
5. what, favorite, clothing brand
6. who, shopping, go, with, usually
7. how often, shopping, go
8. where, good place, this city, shop
9. you, good, deal, getting
10. where, groceries, buy
11. do, ever, subway, products, buy
12. which, better, a big supermarket, an outdoor, traditional market
13. do, sometimes, junk food, snacks or pop, buy
14. what, do, before, shopping, go
15. where, a good place, buy, women's clothes
16. where, a good place, buy, cheap shoes
17. where, I, buy, computer parts
18. Where, I, shopping, go, foreign friend
19. (statement) tell, gift, bought, friend/did, friend, like
20. what, like, buy, foreign brand/where, buy, it

Lesson 03

Part I – Conversation: General Questions – How

1. you, how, study, English
2. you, how, come, the university
3. you, how, make, friends, usually
4. you, how, clean, your room
5. you, how, spend, usually, your vacation
6. you, how
7. you, how, feel, today
8. your parents, how
9. the weather, will, this evening, how
10. your classes, this semester, how
11. your classes, difficult, how
12. you, hard, how, study, usually
13. you, like, how much, your name
14. city tap water, clean, how
15. you, miss, how much, your high school days
16. you, find, how, information, your studies
17. you, feel, how, the Korean president
18. you, hear, how, world news
19. you, contact, usually, how, your friends
20. you, hear, how, your old friends

Part Ⅱ – Conversation: Brand Awareness Questions

1. your favorite brand, clothing, what
2. you, why, like, Nike clothes
3. you, wearing, right now, any Nike clothes
4. Nike, expensive
5. you, buy, Nike clothes, usually, where
6. your favorite fast food chain, what
7. one, where, nearby, that is
8. me, tell, the food, there
9. they, have, any, special events, discounts, or
10. when, the last time, there, you, went
11. you, watch, TV, how often
12. your favorite TV personality, who
13. your favorite TV personality, any commercials, been
14. you, ever, purchased, a product, the commercial, because, a TV star, or, singer,
15. you, ever, met, a famous person, talk, him (her)
16. your favorite cell phone brand, what/why
17. you, buy, products, cheap, where, can
18. your favorite TV commercial, me, tell
19. you, know, any brand songs
20. your favorite brand, what/you, like, so much, it, why

Lesson 04

Part I – Conversation: General Questions

1. you, boyfriend/girlfriend, have
2. you, pets, have, any
3. you, what, your bag, have
4. you, what kind, MP3s, home, music
5. you, usually, what, do, subway
6. you, often, cook
7. you, classes, have, yesterday
8. you, a movie, see, last weekend
9. you, dance, ever, in front of people
10. you, shopping, go, this weekend
11. you, how often, a movie theater, go
12. you, how often, clothes, buy
13. you, how often, sports, play
14. you, how often, to eat, go out
15. you, how many times, text messages, send, every day
16. you, how many countries, have, visited
17. you, how much time, studying, spend
18. you, how much time, exercising, spend
19. you, how many, have, brothers and sisters
20. you, how many times, public transportation, take, every day

Part Ⅱ – Conversation: Jobs

1. you, job, ever, have
2. minimum wage, how much, Korea
3. part time job, what, most popular, college students
4. you, interested, internship, doing
5. company, which, want, work
6. you, to get, a job, do
7. you, what, qualities, want, to have, future jobs
8. you, a trader, be, think, good job
9. you, what kind, job, to have, want
10. your strong points, what
11. you, foreign company, want, work
12. you, to work, want, abroad
13. you, to go, want, graduate school
14. most important thing, to consider, what, you, choose, a job, when
15. you, to work, like, office, all the time
16. you, introduce, please –statement
17. you, why, applying, this job
18. you, most consider, you, apply, a job, when
19. you, what, have, skills, this job
20. me, tell, your work experience –statement

Lesson 05

Part I – Conversation: Foreign Culture

1. you, have, foreign friends
2. you, where, meet, can, foreigners, Korea
3. you, foreign holiday, which, most, like
4. you, country, which, like, visit
5. your opinion, what, Japan
6. Germany, what, famous
7. food, which, country, famous
8. you, feel, how, foreign students, Korea
9. well-known, which, city, shopping, world
10. Korean food, which, popular, foreigners
11. you, like, western food
12. you, watch, foreign movies, how, often
13. you, read, foreign novels
14. you, have, what, image, the Middle East
15. we, how, can, make, foreign friends
16. you, like, foreign dramas
17. you, want, which language, study, English, other than
18. you, where, want, go, your honeymoon
19. country's people, which, similar, Koreans
20. foreigners, how, feel, Korea

Part Ⅱ – Conversation: Travel

*** Ask partner 1-8, then switch and review ***

1. you, where, traveled, recently
2. you, who, go
3. how, the trip
4. you, how, travel
5. money, how much, you, spend, the trip
6. you, what, do, there
7. you, when, go, there
8. you, want, go, there, again
9. you, want, travel, this summer vacation
10. most popular, where, sightseeing place, Korea
11. you, what, need, pack, traveling
12. good time, when, travel
13. you, like, package trips, travel agencies
14. you, like, drive, a car, travel, when
15. you, usually, try, traditional foods, travel, when
16. Korean activities, what kind, you, recommend, would, foreigners
17. you, where, get, can, travel information
18. most important thing, do, what, you, decide, travel, new places, when
19. you, usually, where, stay, a trip
20. you, ever, stayed, a youth hostel

Lesson 06

Part I – Conversation: Computer

1. you, your own computer, have
2. you, heard, a Netbook
3. you, use, what, for, a computer
4. you, use, a computer, when, first
5. which company, computers, famous
6. good place, where, buy, a computer
7. you, use, which company's internet service
8. you, study, computer languages, interested
9. you, use, which software program, editing documents
10. you, any antivirus programs, have, your computer
11. you, spend, how much time, use, a computer
12. you, listen, music, your computer
13. your computer, how old
14. what brand, you, have, computer
15. you, any computer certificates, have
16. you, computer games, like
17. your computer, who, fix, it, broken, when
18. you, download, ever, music, Internet
19. you, chat, ever, your friends, Internet
20. you, have, your own homepage

Part II – Conversation: Free Time

1. you, do, you, free time, have, when
2. you, like, go, the theater
3. movies, what kinds, you, like
4. you, like, read, books
5. you, regularly, read, newspapers
6. you, ever, watched, without a translation, English movies
7. you, like, musical instruments, play
8. musical instrument, what, you, can, play
9. you, do, what, you, home, alone, when
10. you, like, cook
11. you, like, alone
12. you, want, what, do, you, a week free, have, if
13. you, regularly, exercise
14. you, think, you, busy
15. you, think, you, your time, well, manage
16. you, spend, who, your time, the most
17. you, spend, where, your time, majority
18. you, think, when, you, wasting, your time
19. you, how much time, spend, study
20. you, wish, you, more, free time, had

Lesson 07

Part I – Conversation: Friends and Parties

1. you, like, parties
2. what kind, party, you, like
3. you, surprise parties, like
4. what kind, party, you, want, try, your friends
5. which, party, you, go, recently
6. where, a good place, hold, a small party
7. you, like, drink, during a party
8. what, you, will, do, your next birthday
9. what, you, usually, buy, your friend's birthday present
10. what, the best birthday gift, you, ever, received
11. how, you, spend, Valentine's Day
12. your family, enjoy, have, a party
13. what, you, do, Parents' Day
14. what, you, do, your friends, on the weekends
15. who, your best friend/where you meet him/her
16. how many, you, have, good friends
17. a man, a woman, can, be friends
18. what, you, do, usually, Christmas Day
19. where, you, usually, buy, gifts, your friends
20. you, ever, bought, a gift, an Internet shopping mall

Part Ⅱ – Conversation: Introducing Korean Culture

1. what, your favorite, part, Korean culture
2. what, you, think, Korean movies
3. what, mountain, you, hiked up, recently
4. you, read, any Korean novels, lately
5. which, Korean newspaper, you, read
6. which, place, Korea, you, want, visit
7. where, a tourist, can, buy, some souvenirs
8. what, musical instruments, famous, Korea
9. you, own, a "Hanbok"
10. what, you, do, Chuseok
11. what, your favorite, Korean holiday
12. what, you, think, the best Korean food
13. when, North and South Korea, will, reunify
14. you, think, that, Korea, a great place, live
15. where, you, can, go, learn, Korean history
16. where, you, want, live, when, you, 40 years old
17. what, some famous, Korean traditional songs
18. where, the most beautiful, place, Korea
19. you, want, go, sightsee, North Korea
20. why, different, North and South Korean cultures

Lesson 08

Part I – Conversation: Stress

1. what, stress
2. what, cause, stress, your life
3. how, you, like, relax
4. what, your most stressful test, recently
5. you, feeling, stressed, these days
6. what, you, do, when, you, really, angry,
7. you, really, busy, these days
8. you, want, work, hard, or, an easy job, have
9. you, like, be, busy
10. you, ever, listen, music, when, you, stressed
11. drinking, alcohol, a good way, reduce, stress
12. you, think, smoking, cause, more stress, or, reduce, stress
13. what, the most stressful job, you, think, of, can
14. you, happy, these days
15. which, more stressful; dating, or, being, single
16. tell, me, a stressful situation, you, experienced
17. who, make, you, feel, the most stress, your daily life
18. which, class, the most stressful, you, this term
19. which, class, the least stressful, you, this term
20. tell, me, some ways, get, rid of, stress

Part Ⅱ – Conversation: Love and Dating

1. you, have, a boyfriend/girlfriend
2. you, ever, a blind date, been on
3. where, a good place, a date, go on
4. any of your friends, married
5. what, the best gift, receive, your girlfriend/boyfriend
6. when, you, want, get, married
7. where, you, can, meet, a good person, date
8. who, should, pay, dinner; the man, the woman, or, they, should, "go Dutch"
9. you, would, marry, rather, a rich, ugly, person, or, a good-looking, poor person
10. when, you, want, have, children/how, many, you, want, have
11. you, ever, loved, someone, but, they, love, didn't, you
12. where, your parents, meet, first
13. what, something, you, really, hate, when, you, dating
14. it, ok, co-workers, date, each other
15. where, you, want, go, your honeymoon
16. what, the perfect date
17. what, your ideal type
18. you, would, like, date, a famous person/who, if so
19. what, the best clothes, wear, a first date
20. if, your parents, your boyfriend/girlfriend, hate, what, you, would, do

Lesson 09

Part I – Conversation: Music

1. what, music, kind of, you, like
2. you, have, an mp3 player
3. how many, you, have, songs, on your computer
4. when, the last time, you, listened to music
5. what, song, you, listen, recently
6. you, like, go, music concerts
7. who, favorite, singer
8. why, you, like, favorite, singer
9. how often, you, listen, favorite, singer's song
10. where, you, music, download
11. which, you, better, like, classic music, jazz music, or
12. you, like, listen, music, before, fall asleep
13. you, like, sing
14. you, favorite, instrument, musical
15. which, you, prefer; listen, songs, sing, songs
16. how often, you, download, songs, Internet
17. you, ever, buy, CDs, these days
18. what, kind, music, you, listen, when, you, angry
19. what, radio program, you, listen
20. me, tell, your favorite song

Part Ⅱ – Conversation: Health

1. you, think, you, healthy
2. you, want, exercise, more
3. you, have, a cold, last winter
4. how, you, relax
5. you, take, a vitamin, everyday
6. how, often, you, fast food, eat
7. you, eat, or, drink, special, something, your health
8. what, Korean food, famous, being a healthy food
9. you, drink, mineral water
10. you, regularly, exercise
11. you, ever, joined, a health club
12. what, kind, exercise, you, do
13. you, ever, done, yoga
14. you, think, you, out of shape
15. you, ever, been, oriental doctor / why, why not
16. what, you, do, you, have, a cold, when
17. you, ever, gone, diet
18. where, buy, medicine
19. what, restaurant, you, like, cooks, healthy food
20. me, tell, how, stay, healthy

Lesson 10

Part I – Conversation: General Hobbies

1. good ______ . how, you, today
2. have, nickname, English
3. your hobbies
4. why, like, hobby
5. where, play, basketball
6. how hard, skiing
7. how long, been, doing, hobby
8. who, usually do, your hobbies with
9. where, best place, go, ice skating
10. what, hobbies, most popular, in your country
11. what new hobby, you, want, take up
12. how much, hobby, cost, to do
13. are, interested in, learning, how, cook
14. do, ever, play, computer games
15. do, like, play, sports
16. what hobbies, good, families, do together
17. what, new hobbies, recommend, I, take up
18. do you think, married, dating, people, need, have, same hobbies
19. what hobbies, too expensive, you, to do
20. what, some really cheap, hobbies

Part Ⅱ – Conversation: Basic Marketing

1. what, some things, to buy, you want
2. what, some things, to buy, you need
3. you, commercials, like / why, why not
4. you, like, advertisements, subway or bus
5. where, like, shop
6. (past tense) – where, buy, shirt
7. do, ever, a product, online, research, before, buy
8. (past tense) – where, buy, shoes
9. do, like, online, shop
10. what, products, like, shop, for
11. have, ever, sell, anything (also ask #12)
12. (past tense) – how, market, what, sold
13. you, think, good salesperson
14. what kind, marketing, on you, most effective
15. you, think, flyers, people, street, hand out
16. favorite, commercial, these days, TV, on
17. much, money, how, usually, spend, shopping, when
18. where, find, information, new, car, about
19. Do, watch, movie previews, theater, or, usually, ignore
20. what, unique, Korean marketing

Lesson 11

Part I – Conversation: Consumer Behavior (Decision Making)

1. (negative) – why, people, always, buy, online, things
2. Which, better, Coke, Pepsi, Chilsung Cider
3. how, feel, Nike
4. do, ever, credit card, use
5. what, something, buy, soon
6. where, shop, prefer
7. why, prefer, shop, you, favorite, store
8. do, use, coupons, mileage cards
9. do, prefer, domestic brands, foreign brands, to buy
10. what, product, research, buying, before
11. where, do, do research, want, buy, product
12. do brand loyalties, any, have
13. how, learn, new products, about
14. (past tense) – why, return, product
15. have, ever, cell phone, repaired
16. how, feel, after, buy, expensive product
17. (future tense) – what, factors, consider, buy, apartment
18. if, had, 1,000,000 won, what, buy
19. what, factors, most important, car, when, buy
20. do, prefer, name brands, saving money, unknown brands, buying

Part II – Conversation: Daily Life

1. what, time, wake up, morning
2. do, always, eat breakfast
3. what, favorite food, for, breakfast
4. (past) what time, come, school
5. where, usually, eat lunch
6. how long, homework, usually take, finish
7. what, hardest, class
8. what, time, go, home
9. what things, enjoy, doing, home
10. do, usually, eat supper, home, or, go out, eat
11. when, take, shower
12. how much, water, drink, every day
13. do, exercise, these days
14. how long, does, take, get home, here
15. how long, does, take, get ready, morning
16. how long, does, take, fall asleep, night
17. do, ever, bed, late
18. do, parents, get angry, stay out, late
19. what kind, house chores, do, home
20. have, ever, cooked, whole family / what, cook

Lesson 12

Part I – Conversation : Consumer Behavior (Understanding the Buyers)

1. why, customers, angry, sometimes, get
2. why, customers, online, search, product information
3. why, customers, return, after buying, products
4. where else, customers, learn, new products
5. why, take, long time, to shop, clothes, but not, snacks
6. is, buy, cell phone, big purchase decision
7. do, sometimes, put off, buy, something, really want
8. kind, shopper, you
9. why, some people, buying products online, hate
10. have, ever, gone, shopping, another country / if so, tell, experience
11. why, men, usually shop, women, faster
12. who, makes, big purchase decisions, family
13. do, ever, impulse, buy
14. why, customers, love, discounts, coupons
15. if, were, manager, how could, learn more, customers
16. do, think, online shoppers, more satisfied, regular shoppers / why, not
17. if, could, open, store, what kind, store, want, open
18. think, customers, too picky, these days
19. do, agree, this, famous expression : customer, right, always
20. where, favorite, shop, place

Part II – Conversation: Technology

1. you, have, smartphone
2. how much, cell phone, bill
3. where, good place, buy, smartphone
4. how, feel, new technology
5. why, new technology, very expensive
6. when, you, want, get, new computer
7. where, good place, learn, new technology
8. what, new tech gadgets, excited, about
9. which, company, famous, creating new, technological, products
10. you, want, have, car, drives, itself
11. you, ever worried, technology, cause problems
12. why, flying, driving, safer
13. how often, use, Internet
14. is, ok, students, study, smartphones
15. what, technology, love, most
16. what, technology, be like, 10 years
17. what, most popular, mobile device, these days
18. why, some people, afraid, new technology
19. you think, good, many people, camera, in society
20. why, people, usually read news, Internet, buying a newspaper, instead

Lesson 13

Part I – Conversation: Distribution Channels

1. what, four basic parts, supply chain
2. what, think, most important part, supply chain
3. do you think, real estate agents, useful
4. ever, travel agent, used
5. why, more expensive, small shops, big retail stores
6. do you think, always right, customer
7. what, favorite, retail store
8. how, Dunkin' Donuts, fresh donuts, everyday, get
9. why, manufacturers, China, move
10. what, favorite, restaurant franchise
11. have, ever, plane tickets, purchased, online
12. why, some people, tickets online, buy, instead, travel agency
13. would you consider, car, Internet, buy
14. why, Korean postal delivery service, fast
15. Busan, manufacturing companies, any
16. where, built, big ships, Korea
17. you, where, buy, screw driver/paper/new computer
18. ever, foreign products, buy
19. Busan, fresh fish, famous, why
20. what, favorite, kind, soju, where, made

Part II – Conversation: Communication

1. how many, text messages, send, every day
2. how, you, usually, contact, friends
3. you, any, social networking sites, use
4. you, think, alcohol, people communicate better, helps
5. you, prefer, communicate, email, phone call
6. when, call, someone, do, call, via home phone, cell phone
7. you, think, Internet, damaging, social relationships
8. who, you, contact, when, problem, product, have
9. where, ask, questions, new product
10. can, secrets, well, keep
11. can, communicate, effectively, English
12. what topics, enjoy, talking about
13. you, hand gestures, use, when, talking
14. who, you, prefer, to confide in, mother, father, another person
15. you, feel, comfortable, giving, speech, in front, people
16. what, some things, should not talk about, a co-worker
17. what, some good ways, new friends
18. you, often talk, classmates
19. why, people, use Facebook, so much, communicate
20. how, communication helpful, in, workplace

Lesson 14

Part I – Conversation: Advertising I

1. commercial, what, favorite, your
2. advertisements, where, usually, see
3. how, new products, learn
4. do, free samples, like, try
5. advertisement style, what, most, like
6. think, TV commercials, interesting
7. advertisements, subway, read, do you
8. often, how, do, take flyers, people, street
9. mileage cards, do, have?
10. company, advertises, which, most, Korea
11. why, Korean supermarkets, have, lot, people, selling, things, each, aisle
12. do, ever, click, banner ads, surfing the Internet
13. do, think, lie, salespeople
14. you, trust, commercials, TV
15. how, feel, salespeople, subway
16. what, company, want, work
17. how, learn, that company
18. where, see, can, advertisement, that company
19. what kind, products, services, does, company, have
20. think, that company, good

Part II – Conversation: "Have you ever..." with Free Responses

1. ever, (be), another country
2. ever, (fly), in, airplane
3. ever, (break up), someone, you loved
4. ever, (argue), your parents
5. ever, (eat), Mexican food
6. ever, (do), martial arts, such, Hapkido
7. ever, (trip), (fall), down, stairs
8. ever, (throw), punch, someone
9. ever, (get), bloody nose
10. ever, (be), ship
11. ever, (do), something, really, embarrassing
12. ever, (lose), something, you, treasured
13. ever, (buy), food, but, discovered you, no money, had
14. ever, (drink), alcohol, too much
15. ever, (stay), up, all night long
16. ever, (give), money, charity
17. ever, (be), car accident
18. ever, (have), to, surgery, have
19. ever, (make), somebody, really mad, you
20. ever, (work), good company

Lesson 15

Part I – Conversation: Advertising II

1. brand, what, favorite, your
2. favorite brand, where, usually, see
3. how, new services, learn
4. do, new products, like, try
5. advertisement style, what, most, like
6. think, subway ads, interesting
7. advertisements, magazines, read, do you
8. often, how, do, try, free samples
9. coupons, do, have, right now
10. company, advertises, which, most, world
11. you, prefer, talk, salesperson, shop, without, help
12. do, ever, visit, online shopping malls
13. you, think, trustworthy, salespeople
14. you, trust, infomercials, TV
15. How, feel, salespeople, street
16. what, product, want, buy
17. how, learn, that product
18. where, see, can, advertisement, that product
19. what kind, features, attributes, does, product, have
20. why, think, that product, good

Part Ⅱ – Conversation: Beauty

1. who, most beautiful person, Korea?
2. you, think, beauty, helps, people, succeed
3. time, you spend, front, mirror, morning
4. you, think, ok, men, makeup, wear
5. some tips, keep, skin, looking young
6. how, feel, tattoos
7. ok, men, earrings, wear
8. what, ideal type, physically
9. you, think, plastic surgery
10. what, some problems with, attractive, being
11. how, feel when, someone stares, you
12. use, regular soap, shower, body wash
13. which, better, smart, attractive
14. you, worry, getting older
15. you, spend, lot, money, beauty or skin–care products
16. you, think, "beauty is only skin deep", means
17. what, "inner beauty"
18. you, think, mother, beautiful, and, father, handsome
19. ok, children, physical appearance, obsessed
20. what, change, your appearance, want

Lesson 16

Part I – Conversation: Products and Features

1. what kind, car, want, buy
2. what feature, most important, when, buy, car
3. what is, best feature, cell phone
4. what is, most useless, feature, cell phone
5. what kind, computer, have
6. you, think, computer, too old / why, not
7. what feature, important, when, buy, umbrella
8. what, most important thing, consider, when, buy, groceries
9. what, like most, apartment
10. what needs to be repaired, remodeled, apartment
11. what should, consider when, shop, for, gift
12. why, some people, buy, used cars, instead, new cars
13. mind, get, hand–me–downs, family
14. how often, buy, new clothes
15. what, some, features, television
16. do you, dictionary application, cell phone, have
17. what, want, buy, soon
18. where can, buy, best, Samsung products
19. what stores, largest selection, goods, have
20. tell, about, favorite, tech gadget

Part II – Conversation: Home

1. how many, people, your apartment, live
2. what, cleanest room, your apartment
3. you, any pets, have
4. what chores, you, do
5. what brand, refrigerator, you, have
6. you, your apartment, like
7. when, you, did, move, your apartment
8. how many, apartments / houses, lived in, have you
9. you, prefer, study, home, school
10. what, you, usually do, home
11. is, old, your apartment building
12. what time, you, usually, home, go
13. how many, computers, you, home, have
14. do you, like, play music, speakers, home
15. how many, do you have, bathrooms, your apartment
16. how, feel, about home
17. do you have, own room, do you share, somebody
18. which, better, living, top floor, bottom floor
19. what color, bedroom walls, are
20. does, a good view, your apartment, have

Lesson 17

Part I – Conversation: The Internet and Online Shopping

1. where, good place, buy, products, online
2. you, often, products, online, buy
3. what kinds, things, good, buy, Internet
4. what kinds, things, difficult, buy, Internet
5. you, online shopping malls, trust
6. you ever, bought, something, online, you, didn't like
7. you, Internet banking, use
8. products, more expensive, Internet
9. what, you, usually, use, Internet, for
10. how often, you use, Internet
11. how long, you, spend, Internet, every day
12. you, take longer, shop, store, or, online
13. you think, Internet shopping, become, more popular, future
14. what, you, think, pop-up ads
15. you, get, lot, spam mail advertisements
16. ever, your email address, companies, give
17. what, website, visit, most
18. you think, it, dangerous, meet people, Internet
19. what, some major advantages, Internet
20. what, some major disadvantages, Internet

Part Ⅱ – Conversation: Community

1. why, neighbors, argue, sometimes
2. what, benefits, knowing, neighbors
3. ever, you, litter
4. have, ever, done, any, work, volunteer
5. are, grade schools, your community, good
6. your community, good parks, have
7. how, health care, your neighborhood
8. you, member, any, online social groups
9. how active, your community
10. do, want, move, another city
11. what, this community, need, improve
12. people, nice, your hometown
13. were you, this city, born and raised
14. you, have, ever, stranger, helped
15. you, have, favorite, local, sports team
16. what, some good places, hang out, your city
17. your hometown, clean environment, have
18. crime, problem, where you live, is
19. is there, English, a lot, used, your community
20. your community, have, unique culture

Lesson 18

Part I – Conversation: University

1. what, your major
2. what, year, you
3. why, you, choose, your major
4. what, qualities, you, need, your major
5. you, enjoy, study, your major
6. how much, you, spend, study, your major
7. what, your, favorite, class
8. which, professor, most difficult
9. (past) how, often, you, here, come, this semester
10. you, any clubs, in the university
11. you, study, usually, the university library
12. who, you, study, usually
13. where, you, eat, usually, lunch
14. what, you, will, do, this vacation
15. how, often, you, hang out, your classmates
16. you, will, come, the university, this vacation, study
17. you, ever, taken off, a semester, the university
18. what, you, plan, do, after, graduation
19. you, talk to, when, you, have, a problem, your university
20. what, classes, you, take, this semester

| 저자약력 |

Corey Allen Ross is an American living in Busan, South Korea since 2003. He is a foreign professor of the Business Administration Department at the Catholic University of Pusan, and he is working on his Ph.D. in marketing at Pusan National University.

코리 알렌 로스 교수는 2003년부터 대한민국 부산에 거주하고 있는 미국인이다. 현재 부산가톨릭대학교 경영학과의 외국인 교수이며 부산대학교에서 마케팅 전공 박사과정을 수료하였다.

Kap Soo Heo is a professor of the Business Administration Department majoring in Human Resource and a Dean of Graduate School at the Catholic University of Pusan. He is responsible for managing all central policies and processes of graduate programs.

허갑수 교수는 부산가톨릭대학교 경영학과의 HR 전공 교수이며 대학원장이다. 대학원 프로그램의 운영과 관련된 정책 수립과 실행과정을 담당하고 있다.

International Marketing and Business English

2015년 3월 1일 1판 1쇄 인쇄
2015년 3월 5일 1판 1쇄 발행

저　자 Corey Allen Ross · Kap Soo Heo
발행인 이수영
발행처 도서출판 **청람**

㉾ 121-811
서울시 마포구 독막로 288(대흥동, 세양상가 109호)
TEL : 02)3272-2601(대)~2　　FAX : 02)3272~2603
E-mail : crbooks@hanmail.net
http://www.crbooks.co.kr

등록 : 2000. 8. 26 제6-0509호

ISBN 978-89-5972-436-9 93320　　[정가 19,000원]